at the cross

Dramatic Resources
For the Easter Season

PLEASE NOTE: IMPORTANT COPYRIGHT INFORMATION

PERMISSION FOR LIVE, NONPROFIT PERFORMANCES OF THESE SCRIPTS IS GRANTED UPON PURCHASE OF THIS BOOK. PERMISSION IS GRANTED TO MAKE ONLY THE NUMBER OF COPIES NEEDED FOR THE REHEARSAL AND PERFORMANCE OF EACH SCRIPT. THESE RIGHTS ARE GRANTED ONLY TO THE PERFORMING GROUP, CHURCH, ORGANIZATION, SCHOOL, OR INDIVIDUAL WHO HAS PURCHASED THIS BOOK. THIS BOOK MAY NOT BE LOANED, GIVEN AWAY, RENTED, OR SOLD TO ANY OTHER PERFORMING GROUP, CHURCH, ORGANIZATION, SCHOOL, OR INDIVIDUAL WHO IS NOT A PART OF YOUR PERFORMING GROUP. ALL OTHER PERFORMANCE RIGHTS REQUIRE PERMISSION IN WRITING FROM THE PUBLISHER.

WORD, INC.
3319 WEST END AVENUE
NASHVILLE, TENNESSEE 37203

© COPYRIGHT 1994 WORD DRAMA (A DIV. OF WORD, INC.)
ALL RIGHTS RESERVED. INTERNATIONAL COPYRIGHT SECURED.
PRINTED IN U.S.A.

Printed by Davis Brothers Publishing Co., Inc., Waco, TX

at the cross

DRAMATIC RESOURCES
FOR THE EASTER SEASON

AND CAN IT BE? BY DEBORAH CRAIG-CLAAR	7
AT THE CROSS BY PHIL LOLLAR	14
BECAUSE HE LIVES BY PHIL LOLLAR	21
CHRIST THE LORD IS RISEN TODAY BY DEBORAH CRAIG-CLAAR	32
GO TO DARK GETHSEMANE BY DEBORAH CRAIG-CLAAR	40
IN THE GARDEN BY DEBORAH CRAIG-CLAAR	44
LET US BREAK BREAD TOGETHER BY PHIL LOLLAR	52
O SACRED HEAD, NOW WOUNDED BY PHIL LOLLAR	65
OH, HOW HE LOVES YOU AND ME BY DEBORAH CRAIG-CLAAR	57
SOFTLY AND TENDERLY BY PHIL LOLLAR	74
WERE YOU THERE? BY PHIL LOLLAR	82
WHEN I SURVEY THE WONDROUS CROSS BY DEBORAH CRAIG-CLAAR	88

EDITED BY KEITH FERGUSON
DESIGNED BY DEWALL POLLEI & COWLEY DESIGN

OTHER WORD DRAMA PUBLICATIONS

DRAMA FOR WORSHIP VOL. 1 LIFE ISSUES	301 0001 487
DRAMA FOR WORSHIP VOL. 2 RELATIONSHIPS	301 0002 483
DRAMA FOR WORSHIP VOL. 3 CHRISTIAN LIVING	301 0003 48X
DRAMA FOR WORSHIP VOL. 4 CONTEMPORARY ISSUES	301 0004 486
DRAMA FOR WORSHIP VOL. 5 HOLIDAY SCENES	301 0005 482
DRAMA FOR WORSHIP VOL. 6 MARRIAGE & FAMILY	301 0007 485
DRAMA FOR WORSHIP VOL. 7 FOR WOMEN ONLY	301 0008 481
DRAMA FOR WORSHIP VOL. 8 THE CHURCH	301 0011 482
DRAMA FOR YOUTH VOL. 1 YOUTH DRAMA	301 0010 486
FOR THOSE WHO HAVE EARS PAUL & NICOLE JOHNSON	301 0006 489
RAISE THE SAIL PAUL & NICOLE JOHNSON	301 0009 488

FOREWORD

AT THE CROSS—*Dramatic Resources for the Easter Season,* is among the most creative, yet useable collections Word Drama has produced to date. This collection uses classic Easter hymns as the basis for dramatic sketches written around the theme of each hymn.

This is a wonderful resource for worship leaders who wish to enrich the congregation's worship experience during the Easter season, as well as bring another dimension to their hymn singing. Churches using traditional or contemporary worship styles will find material here that will work. These sketches can be used in conjunction with choir, congregation, soloists, or instrumentalists. Most of the sketches stand alone on their own dramatic merits as well. Also, while the focus of this collection is Easter, the sketches are certainly not limited to that season.

The hymns used as titles range from 16th century classics, such as "O Sacred Head, Now Wounded," to contemporary standards like "Because He Lives." Dramatic settings range from Biblical scenes to contemporary living rooms. The collection includes monologues, Reader's Theater material, and dramatic sketches with dialogue.

Bringing this material to life are two excellent writers, **Deborah Craig-Claar** and **Phil Lollar**. Deborah and Phil both bring a wealth of theatrical experience to this project, as well as a good understanding of the needs of today's church. Most importantly, their skills are undergirded by an appreciation for liturgy and worship.

It is our hope that this collection will provide many meaningful worship experiences for your church.

WORD DRAMA

And Can It Be?

TEXT: Charles Wesley
MUSIC: Thomas Campbell

This text reveals Charles Wesley's genius as a hymn writer—to make the theological so exciting and emotional.

In their book, *Sing with Understanding,* Harry Eskew and Hugh T. McElrath list the following traits of a Wesleyan hymn. "And Can It Be" is an excellent example.

1) Replete with doctrine.
2) Full of scriptural allusion.
3) Expressive of a passionate Christian experience, while being free of vulgarity and excess.
4) Simple, direct, and evangelistic.
5) Mystical and illuminating in the way that Wesley talks directly to God as friend, a quality that makes his hymns timeless and universal in their appeal.

* © Copyright 1980 Broadman Press

And can it be that I should gain
An interest in the Savior's blood?
Died He for me, who caused His pain?
For me, who Him to death pursued?

REFRAIN:
Amazing love! how can it be
That Thou, my God shouldst die for me?

He left His Father's throne above,
So free, so infinite His grace!
Emptied Himself of all but love,
And bled for Adam's helpless race!
'Tis mercy all, immense and free,
For, O my God, it found out me.

Long my imprisoned spirit lay
Fast bound in sin and nature's night.
Thine eye diffused a quick'ning ray;
I woke the dungeon flamed with light!
My chains fell off, my heart was free,
I rose, went forth, and followed Thee.

No condemnation now I dread :
Jesus, and all in Him is mine!
Alive in Him, my living Head, And clothed in righteousness divine,
Bold I approach th'eternal throne,
And claim the crown, thru Christ my own.

And Can It Be?
A Dramatic Sketch
by
Deborah Craig-Claar

SYNOPSIS
Two pairs of guards and their prisoners—one Biblical, one contemporary—write letters from jail. In the first sequence, the apostle Paul and a Jerusalem jailer react to the events following Paul's incarceration for preaching to Gentiles (Acts 21-23). In the following sequence, a newly-converted prisoner on death row and a guard recount a recent prison riot. In both cases, we discover the guards are actually the ones "imprisoned" and the prisoners are the ones who are "free." The two sequences can be used separately (do just the left side of the page or just the right side) for short dramatic introductions to the hymn, or the full piece can provide a unique Biblical-contemporary perspective. The two sequences can follow one another (do just the left half of the page, followed by just the right half), or you can intersperse them (as formatted in the script), fluctuating between Biblical and contemporary as each character speaks. Because the drama is in the form of letters, it can be performed several different ways: the actors can memorize and fully perform the pieces, they can read the letters as they write, or the letters can be prerecorded and played (as if we hear the characters' thoughts) as the actors write silently on stage. It is recommended that the first two stanzas of "And Can It Be?" be sung before the sketch, and that stanzas three and four follow the sketch. The third stanza is the primary basis for this dramatic rendering.

| Performance Time: | 6—7 minutes |

WORSHIP USES
General; Forgiveness themes. An excellent piece to introduce "And Can It Be," if the hymn is unfamiliar.

WORD MUSIC RESOURCES
- SATB Anthem, arr. by Kurt Kaiser, #3010629168

SETTING/PROPS
The scene can be performed on an empty stage. All four actors should have a place to sit. Paul should be in shackles (a long chain, so he can easily write); his jailer might have a large ring of keys. Ray is in prison garb; his guard is in uniform with weapons (if possible). All four need to have hard surfaces (books, pieces of wood, etc.) on which to write, paper or parchment, and writing utensils.

CHARACTERS
PAUL, the apostle, presently in prison

JAILER, a coarse man, but strongly affected by Paul's spirit

RAY, a criminal on death row who has recently converted

GUARD, a simple man who harbors a great deal of anger

PAUL:
My dear brother...

JAILER:
To Hiram...

PAUL:
Grace to you and peace from God our Father and the Lord Jesus Christ. I thank my God for you, for your perseverance and your steadfastness of hope.

JAILER:
I know it's been a long time since we've seen each other. For some reason I've been thinking about old acquaintances lately.

PAUL:
I write to you from a prison in Jerusalem, where I am being held for preaching Jesus Christ to the Gentiles.

JAILER:
I've been assigned to the dungeon prison in the Roman barracks in Jerusalem. It's not much different than the prison in Antioch, except colder and dirtier... if that's possible...

PAUL:
I was put in chains by the Romans, to keep me from being killed by an angry crowd of Jews. It has been several hours since sunset, and I continue to hear the shouting and crying above me in the streets. Sometimes I marvel at the anger still in the world...

RAY:
Dear Frank...

GUARD:
Al...

RAY:
How can I thank you for this past year—for the friend you've been. You've always stood firm, you've never wavered...

GUARD:
Yeah. It's me. Surprise. No, I haven't fallen off the face of the earth, although at times I've wondered if _you_ have...

RAY:
It's my thirty-seventh month at Angola, but time just seems to stand still here, especially on death row.

GUARD:
I'm workin' the graveyard shift again at Angola. Yeah. Stuck. And what a hell hole. I might as well be one of the inmates.

JAILER:
And now, as if things weren't black enough, another one of those itinerant holy men came through today. For someone who claims to only preach love, he certainly stirs up hate. The Romans want him exiled, the Jews seem to want him dead. Strange. What a world it's become when being chained in a prison is the safest place for someone . . .

PAUL:
If the truth be known, my brother, I almost welcome the silence of this cell. I even welcome the shackles. Sometimes God must force me to be still and examine the storm that always seems to swirl around me. And how fitting to lift my hands to Him, and feel the weight of earthly chains—knowing I have long ago been set free from my sin through Christ Jesus . . .

RAY:
There was a riot yesterday. You probably heard about it in the news. Strange. No one was trying to escape; three guys just went berserk. Nine more ended up dead. (*pause*) With all the pent-up hate and anger around here I guess I should be surprised it doesn't happen more often.

GUARD:
And now another riot. I managed to keep clear, but I swear, I wish we'd just let the scum all kill each other off. The world would sure be a better place.

RAY:
In your last letter you asked if the solitude and endless rows of steel bars ever got to me. In all honesty I must tell you no, not anymore. I don't mind the separation from the world. The world and what I did with it is how I got here. Funny. But even the bars seem to remind me that I'm free from all that now . . . ever since you helped me find Jesus last year . . .

JAILER:
There is this prisoner that both the Romans and Jews seem to hate—Paul is his name, I believe . . .

GUARD:
And not only do I have the scum to contend with, but also certified fruitcakes—like this one guy named Ray . . .

PAUL:
There's no one else in the prison tonight, except the jailer . . .

RAY:
There's been a new guard assigned to my cell block . . .

JAILER:
What a strange man he is . . .

GUARD:
Absolutely crazy . . .

PAUL:
He seems sad . . . and so alone . . .

RAY:
He's very bitter . . . and full of rage. Just like I used to be.

JAILER:
He came to the jail willingly. He even <u>blessed</u> those that put the shackles on. Most prisoners curse and yell the entire time about getting out. But this Paul is strangely quiet; almost . . . content. Sometimes I honestly wonder if he knows where he is . . .

GUARD:
I've quit tryin' to figure Ray out. I mean, here's a guy who's got nobody on the outside. He shoots somebody during a robbery, gets first degree, and now has maybe three months left. But every morning when I check on him, he seems almost . . . <u>happy</u>. Like he's looking forward to somethin'. Crazy. Absolutely crazy. This place must be gettin' to both of us . . .

PAUL:
I've tried talking to this jailer, but I'm not sure how much he's heard . . .

RAY:
Having a conversation with this guard has been almost impossible, but I've kept trying . . .

JAILER:
This prisoner keeps telling me about a man who came and took the punishment for my sins—even died. For me. This Paul said there is no condemnation for those who believe this man. And I've never even met Him. Now how can that be . . . ?

GUARD:
Now how can this be . . . this jive Ray keeps handin' me . . .'bout some guy a long time ago forgivin' all the trash I've heaped onto my life? Some guy . . . that I don't even know . . . lovin' me . . . in spite of everything. "No condemnation," Ray said. Yeah. Right. That ain't the way justice in this world is doled out . . .

(*The following lines are said rapidly, overlapping, almost as if it is one thought.*)

PAUL:
I wish I could help him, he seems so . . .

RAY:
He seems . . .

JAILER:
Sometimes I feel so . . .

GUARD:
It's like I'm always . . .

ALL:
. . . trapped.

(*Pause, then quietly, also overlapping.*)

PAUL:
Remember him in your prayers . . .

RAY:
Pray for him . . .

JAILER:
Well, it's of little matter to
anyone . . .

GUARD:
So who gives a rip . . . Nobody I
know . . .

(*Another pause, then with a tempo and volume increase.*)

PAUL:
So, my dear brother, until I am able
to write again . . .

RAY:
Well I'd better be going . . .

JAILER:
I must return to my watch. Perhaps,
this year, I will hear from you . . .

GUARD:
That's it, I guess. Call sometime . . . if
you remember . . .

PAUL:
Please greet the brethren in the
abundant love of the Lord Jesus . . .

RAY:
In the amazing love of our Lord . . .

JAILER:
Until another time . . .

GUARD:
Later . . .

PAUL:
Grace . . .

RAY:
Peace . . .

PAUL & RAY:
. . . be with you.

(*At this point, the lights fade and the congregation sings the third and fourth stanzas of "And Can It Be?"*)

At the Cross

(*Alas! And Did My Savior Bleed*)

TEXT: Isaac Watts; Ralph E. Hudson, Refrain
MUSIC: Ralph E. Hudson

This hymn was included in Watts' collection, *Hymns and Spiritual Songs* (1707). Over the years, all of the stanzas have been altered in some way. The fourth line of the first stanza originally read "For such a worm as I," and has been changed in many collections to read, "For sinners such as I," as it appears here. This is done for literary purposes and should not be regarded as any kind of theological compromise. It is interesting to note that Watts' writing was very descriptive and dramatic and has often been subject to alteration in an effort to soften some of the extreme qualities. Watts was a Congregational minister who helped to create two important types of English hymns—personal devotional expressions and scriptural paraphrases.

Ralph Hudson's words for the refrain appeared with the music in 1885 in his collection, *Songs of Peace, Love and Joy*. While Hudson is credited with the refrain, it is probable that the refrain arose out of the camp meeting tradition of the late 19th century.

Alas! and did my Savior bleed?
And did my Sov'reign die?
Would He devote that sacred head
For sinners such as I!

Was it for crimes that I have done
He groaned upon the tree?
Amazing pity! grace unknown!
And love beyond degree!

Well might the sun in darkness hide
And shut His glories in,
When Christ, the mighty Maker died
For man the creature's sin.

But drops of grief can ne'er repay
The debt of love I owe:
Here, Lord, I give myself away—
'Tis all that I can do!

REFRAIN:
At the cross, at the cross where I first saw the light
And the burden of my heart rolled away—
It was there by faith I received my sight,
And now I am happy all the day!

At the Cross
A Dramatic Sketch
by Phil Lollar

SYNOPSIS
A young person feels the hymn *At the Cross* is boring and meaningless. Three people prove him wrong by revealing the effect the hymn had on their lives.

| Performance Time: | 5-6 minutes with hymn |

WORSHIP USES
Easter season and General worship

SETTING/PROPS
The normal church sanctuary. No props.

CHARACTERS
WORSHIP LEADER
YOUNG PERSON (male or female—your choice)
MAN #1
MAN #2
THE CONGREGATION

Author's Note: This sketch should be played out during the course of a normal service. If it is done properly, people may not catch on right away that it's a sketch. But do let the pastor, the choir director and the other church leaders know—just in case.

(*The stage and sanctuary lights are up full.* <u>For the best effect, the worship leader should lead a hymn or praise chorus just prior to this one.</u> *Once that song is finished, the WORSHIP LEADER speaks to the congregation.*)

WORSHIP
LEADER: Please be seated . . . (*he waits while they do*) Now take a hymnal and turn to hymn number (*insert the number from your hymnal for "At the Cross."*)

          (*The piano or organ provides the intro, and the congregation sings the first verse.*)

ALL: "Alas! and did my Savior bleed? And did my Sovereign die?
Would He devote that sacred head for such a worm as I?
At the cross, at the cross where I first saw the light,
And the burden of my heart rolled away,
It was there by faith I received my sight
And now I am happy all the day!"

(*During this verse, the worship leader notices something he doesn't like in the audience. After the verse is complete, he stops the song.*)

WORSHIP LEADER: Excuse me! . . . Excuse me, please! Could we just stop for a moment? Just for a moment, please . . . (*the music and singing dies down*) I'm sorry everyone, but I'm seeing something out there that I just can't ignore . . . (*he looks straight at a young person [male or female—your choice]—perhaps even moves toward them—and says*) You there—is there something wrong?

YOUNG PERSON: (*looks around, disbelieving*) Uh . . .

WORSHIP LEADER: Yes (*young person's real name*), I'm talking to *you*. Is there something wrong?

YOUNG PERSON: (*nervously*) W-wrong?

WORSHIP LEADER: Yes, *wrong*. While we were singing, you were sitting there, slouched in your seat, rolling your eyes like this was the most painful thing in the world for you to endure. Don't you like this song?

(*The YOUNG PERSON slowly stands.*)

YOUNG PERSON: Well . . . to be honest with you . . . not really.

WORSHIP LEADER: Why not?

YOUNG
PERSON: I dunno . . . the tune's okay, I guess . . . But, it's just that . . . well, the song is kinda . . . *boring*, you know?

WORSHIP
LEADER: Boring.

YOUNG
PERSON: I mean, the words are really flowery—(*melodramatically*) "Alas! and did my Savior bleed?" (*normal*) It sounds like a melodrama. And then there's these other lines that I just don't relate to, like . . . (*looks*) Uh, yeah: ". . . for such a worm as I" . . . and . . . "Was it for crimes that I have done . . ." I mean, that's kinda strong, isn't it?

(*Suddenly, from another part of the congregation, a man stands.*)

MAN #1: I don't think so.

(*Everyone turns to look at him.*)

YOUNG
PERSON: You don't?

MAN #1: No. As a matter of fact, this song means a lot to me—because I know what it means to be a worm.

YOUNG
PERSON: You do?

MAN #1: Yeah. See, I'm a recovering addict.

YOUNG
PERSON: You are?!

MAN #1: Yeah—surprised, huh?

YOUNG
PERSON: Well, I—

MAN #1: (*interrupts*) I started using drugs to cover up an aching emptiness I felt inside. I thought as long as they did that, I was fine. But by the time I was 25, I looked like a corpse . . . I had nothing. I lived alone in a filthy, slum apartment. I had no furniture, no telephone. I wore the same old clothes every day . . . It was terrible. So I tried to kick it with counseling, psychiatry, methadone. But nothing worked . . . I was completely helpless—and without hope . . . Then one night, I was strung out, and I staggered past a rescue mission . . . above the door was a sign that said: "LET GO AND LET JESUS" . . .

I went inside. There was a service going on, and they were singing this song—that's why it means so much to me. I saw a little cross behind the pulpit, and I got down on my knees before it and I prayed: "Dear Jesus, I've tried everything to get off of drugs. I don't know what else to do. I'm lost. Please . . . help me." And I suddenly realized that that aching emptiness wasn't there anymore. Something—a small spark of *life* —had taken its place. So, I wrapped up the drugs, tied a rock to them and threw them into the river. Then I thanked Jesus with all my heart . . . Oh, it hasn't been easy. I still struggle. But whenever I'm really tempted, I just remember that Jesus took this worm—the scum of the earth, completely undeserving—and turned him into a butterfly.

(*Right then, from a different part of the auditorium, another man stands.*)

MAN #2: He did the same thing for a criminal!

(*Everyone turns and looks.*)

YOUNG
PERSON: A criminal?!

MAN #2: Yeah . . . I was a thief—armed robbery. Held up liquor stores and gas stations . . . One night, I pulled a stocking over my head and hit an electronics store . . . at first the owner thought it was a joke—until I pointed the gun right at his face and pulled the trigger . . . but it jammed. This made me mad, so I smashed the gun butt over the guy's head, cleaned out the cash register and split . . . the police caught me a couple of blocks away—the guy had a hidden alarm . . . I was convicted and sent to the county prison . . . six months into my sentence, the guard tells me I have a visitor. I go to the room . . . and there across the table sits the guy from the electronics store. I figure he's here to gloat . . . only . . . he doesn't. Instead, he wants to know how I'm doing . . . he said God put me on his heart, and he wanted to pray for me . . . I thought he was pulling my leg . . . but then, I looked at his face . . . and a tear rolled down his cheek . . . He prayed, and gave me a Bible . . . (*pause*) The next Sunday, I went to Chapel . . . it was the first time I'd been to church since I was a kid . . . They were singing that song . . . and I realized what "Amazing pity! Grace unknown! And love beyond degree!" was all about.

(*There is a long beat, then . . .*)

YOUNG
PERSON: Who are you guys trying to kid?

MAN #1:   (*uncomfortably*) W-what do you mean?

MAN #2:   (*also uncomfortably*) Yeah, uh, what are you talking about?

YOUNG
PERSON: You know what I'm talking about! (*points to MAN #1*) You're (*actor's real name*) and you live at (*address*)! (*points at MAN #2*) And <u>you're</u> (*second actor's real name*) and you live at (*address*)! I've known both of you ever since I was a kid! You never used drugs, and <u>you</u> never robbed anybody! Neither one of you is a worm or a criminal!

WORSHIP
LEADER: You're wrong, (*young person's real name*).

YOUNG
PERSON: What?

WORSHIP
LEADER: They *are* worms and criminals. So am I. So is everyone in this room—including *you*.

YOUNG
PERSON: What are you talking about?

WORSHIP
LEADER: <u>Sin</u>. Don't you see? <u>That's</u> what makes us worms and criminals. Every one of us has a story—<u>multiple</u> stories—about our sins. Oh, maybe they're not as dramatic as the ones we just heard, but they're just as valid.

YOUNG
PERSON: What's yours?

WORSHIP
LEADER: You really want to know?

YOUNG
PERSON: Yes!

WORSHIP
LEADER: (*smiles*) All right . . . I was walking home from school when I was eight years old . . . and passed by my neighbor's apricot tree . . . I knew she didn't want me to pick any of them . . . but I did anyway . . . I had apricots at home—all I could eat and better than the ones I picked . . . but I still took hers . . . just because they were there . . . and just because she didn't want me to.

YOUNG
PERSON: That's it?

WORSHIP
LEADER: There have been others since then, but that was the first I remember.

YOUNG
PERSON: But . . . they were just apricots!

WORSHIP
LEADER: It doesn't make any difference! Sin is sin—whether it's stealing apricots, robbing an electronics store, or abusing your body with drugs. It's all the same to God. He can't allow it—<u>any</u> of it! Each one of us deserves to die. But God loved us so much, He sent His Son to die in our place. Do you realize how <u>incredible</u> that is? That's what this hymn is all about. Isaac Watts, the writer, found it so amazing that Jesus—the creator and Lord of the universe—would sacrifice Himself, just so that the very people who spit in His face could live with Him in eternity . . . so that worms and criminals like us could know "love beyond degree" . . . (*pause*) Understand?

YOUNG
PERSON: Yeah, I understand.

WORSHIP
LEADER: So you think maybe we can sing this hymn now with a little more feeling and meaning?

YOUNG
PERSON: (*smiles*) Sure.

WORSHIP
LEADER: Good! (*to the congregation*) Let's all stand and sing it together.

(*The piano or organ provides the intro, and the congregation sings the first verse.*)

Because He Lives

TEXT: Gloria and William J. Gaither
MUSIC: William J. Gaither
© Copyright 1971 by William J. Gaither. All Rights Reserved. Used by permission of Gaither Music Company.

This contemporary classic has become a standard and appears in many different denominational and ecumenical hymnals. The text speaks about a personal faith in Christ, as well as the theological importance of the resurrection. In fact, the tune was given the name RESURRECTION by the Gaithers when it was included in a hymnal for the first time, the *Baptist Hymnal*, 1975. The Gaithers provided this background information at that time.

Although history has revealed that this world has never been very stable, it seems that our century has been especially a time of upheaval and crisis. Our world is a planet filled with injustices, betrayals of national and personal trust, bigotry, greed, and immorality, situated on a nuclear powder keg, the fuse of which is well within the reach of men who may be lacking in sound moral judgement and personal integrity. It was into this world at such a time that we were bringing our third little baby. Assassinations, riots, drug traffic, and war monopolized the headlines.

It was in the midst of this kind of uncertainty that the assurance of the Lordship of the Risen Christ blew across our troubled minds like a cooling breeze in a parched desert. Holding our tiny son in our arms we were able to write:

> God sent His Son,
> they called Him Jesus,
> He came to love, heal and forgive;
> He lived and died to buy my pardon,
> An empty grave is there to prove my Savior lives.
>
> *REFRAIN:*
> Because He lives
> I can face tomorrow,
> Because He lives
> all fear is gone;
> Because I know
> He holds the future,
> And life is worth the living
> just because He lives.
>
> How sweet to hold
> a newborn baby,
> And feel the pride and joy he gives;
> But greater still the calm assurance,
> This child can face uncertain days because He lives.
>
> And then one day,
> I'll cross the river,
> I'll fight life's final war with pain;
> And then as death gives way to victory,
> I'll see the lights of glory and I'll know He lives.

Because He Lives
A Dramatic Sketch
by Phil Lollar

SYNOPSIS
Three generations of a family are faced with crises and, through them, learn something about the hope of the resurrection. **NOTE: This piece should be sung by a small Ensemble or the Church Choir. Only on the last verse will the Congregation sing.

Performance Time:	8-10 minutes with hymn

WORSHIP USES
Easter or General worship

WORD MUSIC RESOURCES
- Studio Series Artist Trax, as recorded by The Bill Gaither Trio #3017119203

SETTING/PROPS
The stage is divided into three parts—two living room sets and one "restaurant" set.

CHARACTERS
DAVE-	Mid 20s
LORI-	Early 20s
BOB-	DAVE'S father, early 50s
JOAN-	DAVE'S mother, early 40s
WAITER-	Mid 20s
OWEN-	DAVE'S grandfather, late 60s
BESS-	DAVE'S grandmother, late 60s
CHOIR	

SCENE ONE

(From the darkness, music begins. A spotlight rises on a small choir, who brings us the chorus of "Because He Lives.")

CHOIR: Because He lives, I can face tomorrow,
Because He lives, all fear is gone;
Because I know He holds the future,
And life is worth the living just because He lives.

(The spot fades on them, and the lights rise centerstage. A young man, DAVE, sits on the stage-right side of a sofa, reading a newspaper. After a few seconds, his wife, LORI, appears, upstage left. She is with child—enormously with child. She waddles onto the stage, unnoticed by her husband, and makes her way to the stage-left side of the sofa, where she attempts to sit down. After several comical tries, she decides there is no graceful way of doing this, so she unceremoniously tumbles onto the sofa and sinks awkwardly into its cushions. Then, just as she gets comfortable, DAVE, who has been completely unaware of her until now, looks up from his paper and says:)

DAVE: Oh, hi, honey. Dinner ready yet?

(A pause, then LORI responds in the only way she is currently capable of responding—she bursts out in an exaggerated sob.)

LORI: *(sobs)* Whaaaaa!!

DAVE: *(sensitively)* Lori, what's the matter?

LORI: *(frustrated)* When is this baby gonna come?!

DAVE: Aw . . . feelin' kinda bad?

LORI: *(sarcastic)* Whatever gave you *that* idea?! You try swallowing a hot air balloon and see how *you* feel!

DAVE: I guess things are pretty rough, huh?

(LORI glares at him.)

LORI: Did you take some sort of stupid question pill this morning? *Yes* things are rough!! I move around like a beached whale . . . my wedding ring will only fit on the tip of my pinkie now . . . my back and lungs feel like I have a Sherman tank permanently parked on 'em . . . And I'm seriously considering moving into the bathroom to save wear and tear on the carpet! . . . I'm a week overdue, David! When is he gonna come!?

DAVE: Well, at the risk of sounding insensitive and stupid again . . . he'll come when he's ready—when it's time.

LORI: Yeah, you're right—that was insensitive and stupid.

DAVE: I'm sorry, sweetheart.

LORI: (*nicer*) I know; me, too . . . (*sighs*) I'm just so impatient! I want it to happen already!

DAVE: Will it help if I rub your back?

LORI: (*almost like a little girl*) Mm-hm.

(*She moves into position and he rubs her back.*)

DAVE: I know you won't believe this . . . but I'm just as anxious to see the little guy as you are . . . to hold him . . . touch his little hands and feet . . .

LORI: You know, we keep saying "him"—what if it's a girl?

DAVE: Okay by me!

LORI: That's easy for you to say—down a little more . . .

DAVE: There?

LORI: Uh-huh . . . that does feel better . . . Did you call your folks?

DAVE: Yeah . . . They're going out to eat tonight.

LORI: Together?

DAVE: Uh-huh.

LORI: That's encouraging, isn't it?

DAVE: Dad thought it was. And I think Mom did, too.

LORI: Oh . . . You think they'll be able to work this out, David?

DAVE: (*shrugs*) I dunno . . . things are still pretty touchy . . . Mom asked me to call Gramps again.

LORI: Are you going to?

DAVE: Yeah . . . although I don't think it'll do any good.

LORI: There's nothing physically wrong with him, is there?

DAVE: No, it's all emotional. For some reason, he just doesn't want to *talk* to anybody about it . . . it's really hard on Granny.

LORI: Poor thing—(*a sudden twinge*)—oh!

DAVE: (*alert*) What's the matter? Did I hurt you?

LORI: No . . . I think . . . I have to go to the bathroom again.

DAVE: You need help?

LORI: Just with getting up. The rest, I've had <u>lots</u> of practice at . . .

(*He helps her up, and she waddles off up left. DAVE again continues talking, first to her, then to himself.*)

DAVE: It's funny . . . can you believe there was ever a time when we <u>didn't</u> want to have children? When we thought the world was so messed up, it wouldn't be fair to bring new life into it? . . . And now, I can't think of anything I want <u>more</u> . . . I still sometimes wonder if we're doing the right thing . . . but, then I think about the miracle that's happening . . . God is making a new . . . <u>life!</u> That is just so amazing! And then I think, if He can do <u>that</u> . . . He can certainly handle everything else that's going on in the world.

(*He thinks on this as LORI re-enters—and it's obvious that all is not well with the world. That bathroom twinge was actually a labor pain—the big moment has finally come.*)

LORI: (*in pain*) Dave . . . Dave, it's time . . .

DAVE: (*still lost in thought*) Time for what, honey?

LORI: (*in pain; sarcastic*) What do you <u>think</u> it's time for?!

DAVE: (*snaps out of it*) Oh! You mean, it's <u>the</u> time!!

(*He rushes to her.*)

LORI: Yes, <u>the</u> time—ooohh!!

DAVE: Okay, now, we'll just take it nice and slow . . . everything is all packed . . . I'll call the doctor and the hospital from the car . . . (*happily, with love*) I guess the little guy's finally ready, huh?

LORI: Yeah—ooohh! (*breathes hard*) But now I'm not sure <u>I</u> am . . . (*suddenly scared*) David, I'm . . . scared . . .

DAVE: (*gently, reassuring*) Shh, no need to be—<u>He's</u> with us . . . Now, c'mon— let's go have a baby . . .

(*He leads her off, upstage right. The lights fade on them. The spotlight hits the choir, who brings us* **verse two** *of the song.*)

CHOIR: How sweet to hold a newborn baby, and feel the pride and joy he gives;
But greater still the calm assurance, this child can face uncertain days because He lives.

(*The spot fades on the choir.*)

SCENE TWO

(*The lights rise stage left. We're in a restaurant. BOB sits at the table. He rubs his hands together nervously, then looks skyward.*)

BOB: (*low, anxious*) <u>Please</u>, God, let this work out.

(*He straightens the silverware, then, after a few seconds, his wife, JOAN, enters from off left. We can tell immediately that something is wrong in this relationship. BOB instantly hops up when he sees her.*)

BOB: Here we are! (*helps her sit*) There.

JOAN: (*reserved*) Thank you.

(*BOB sits. There is a long, uncomfortable pause.*)

JOAN: (*looks around*) They've changed the interior of this place. It's darker.

BOB: Yeah. I think I liked it better when it was brighter.

JOAN: I like it better now.

BOB: Dark is good, too . . . uh, they haven't changed the menu, though. It's still just as fabulous.

JOAN: Where <u>is</u> the menu?

BOB: Uh, well, the waiter has it. I already ordered for us—chateaubriand.

JOAN: (*stiffening*) You ordered for both of us?

BOB: Um . . . yeah.

JOAN: How did you know what I wanted?

BOB: Well, uh, I . . . remembered that you always liked chateaubriand.

JOAN: I <u>never</u> liked chateaubriand—<u>you</u> did.

BOB: Oh . . . uh, well, you want me to get the waiter?

JOAN: No, never mind.

BOB: It's no trouble. Let me just flag him down—

JOAN: (*firmly*) Bob, I said <u>never mind</u>!

(*He sees her expression and slowly relaxes.*)

BOB: Okay ... (*a pause, almost pleading*) Joan ... I'm trying really hard here.

JOAN: I know you are, but you never <u>listen</u>!

BOB: You're right, I'm sorry, I ... I just want tonight to be perfect, that's all ... I thought it might ... make up for things ...

JOAN: (*a curt laugh; shakes her head*) That is <u>so</u> like you ... you think one perfect night can make up for everything.

BOB: No, not everything ... just ... <u>some</u> things ...

JOAN: Yeah ... well, it's a little late for that, isn't it?

BOB: I hope not ... I hope it's <u>never</u> too late for us.

JOAN: You should have thought of that before you—(*stops herself*)

BOB: (*a deep sigh*) Joan ... it was almost a year ago ... it was one night, and it was wrong—<u>I</u> was wrong. I've asked God to forgive me, and I believe He <u>has</u> ... Can't <u>you</u> find it in your heart to do the same?

JOAN: (*painfully, controlled*) It <u>wasn't</u> just one night, Bob!

BOB: Yes, it <u>was</u>!

JOAN: Maybe with <u>her</u>—but it's been <u>years</u> of neglect with <u>me</u>! ... Your "fling" was ... devastating ... but, she was just the last straw! (*she blinks back tears*) For me, the past 10 years of marriage has been one—long—<u>hurt</u>! That's something you don't seem to understand!

BOB: Yes, I do! I <u>know</u> I've hurt you! And if I could take back the last 10 years, I <u>would</u>—in a heartbeat! But, I can't! Joan ... I don't have the words to tell you how much you mean to me, and how deeply sorry I am for the way I've treated you ... all I can tell you is that I love you ... and I want our marriage to <u>work</u>.

(*There is a long pause as she looks at him.*)

JOAN: (*still hurt*) I want to believe you ... but it's very ... difficult.

BOB: I know ... so maybe we shouldn't rely on <u>ourselves</u> to do this ... Maybe we should give it to God ... (*searchingly*) Okay?

JOAN: (*a pause*) It's . . . still going to take time.

BOB: Then <u>let</u> it take time . . . I'm not going anywhere. And neither is God.

(*She nods hesitantly, and he caresses her face gently. A pause, and then waiter approaches, carrying telephone.*)

WAITER: Excuse me, sir?

BOB: Yes?

WAITER: Are you Mr. Johnson?

BOB: That's right.

WAITER: You have a phone call. (*he sets down the phone and leaves*)

BOB: Thank you . . . (*picks up the phone*) Hello? . . . David? . . . She <u>is</u>?! All right, we'll be right there! . . . Don't worry about us! You just take care of her! Bye!

JOAN: Is Lori—?

BOB: In labor! And from the way David sounded, it's not gonna be very long! C'mon, we've gotta go!

(*They get up and put on their coats.*)

JOAN: I want to call my folks.

BOB: We'll do that from the hospital!

JOAN: (*realizes; overwhelmed*) Oh, Bob . . . I'm gonna be a <u>grandmother</u>!

BOB: (*smiles at her*) I know!

JOAN: I . . . hope I can handle it!

BOB: (*sincerely*) You'll handle it like you handle everything else—with strength . . . and grace . . . and love. (*beat*) That's why I married you.

(*another pause as they look at each other*)

JOAN: We'd better go. . .

(*They exit together, stage left. The lights fade on them. The spotlight hits the choir, who brings us* **verse one** *of the song.*)

CHOIR: God sent His Son, they called Him Jesus, He came to love, heal and forgive;
He lived and died to buy my pardon, an empty grave is there to prove my Savior lives.

(*The spot fades on the choir.*)

SCENE THREE

(*The lights rise stage right. Sitting in a chair is OWEN. He does nothing, just sits and stares, in a deep depression. After a few seconds, his wife, BESS enters from stage right with a tray of food and sets it on a small table next to him.*)

BESS: Here we go! I thought you might like a little minestrone soup.

OWEN: (*a deep sigh*) I'm not hungry.

BESS: You sure? It's really good! (*no response*) Well, I'm gonna have some . . . (*she takes a bowl and starts to eat when the phone rings*) Ooo, wouldn't you know it? Happens every time! (*she puts down the bowl and answers the phone*) Hello? . . . Oh, hello, sweetheart! (*to OWEN*) It's Joanie, dear. (*back into the phone*) She is!? Right now? . . . That's wonderful!! . . . (*mood change*) Well . . . I don't know . . . I wouldn't count on it, honey . . . No, not really . . . Well, give them all our love . . . okay, bye. (*hangs up, excited*) Owen! Lori is finally having her baby! Isn't that great!?

OWEN: (*can only muster another sigh*)

(*BESS moves to his chair and kneels next to him.*)

BESS: (*gently*) Hey, mister! Didn't you hear? A new baby! Another miracle is happening while we talk—and right in our own family!

OWEN: I don't believe in miracles anymore, Bess.

BESS: (*mild teasing*) Oh, you ol' grouchy-grouch! I tell you what—why don't we go down there and take a look at our new great-grandchild?

OWEN: (*looks at her, pats her hand*) You go on ahead.

BESS: (*upset*) Owen Taylor! Don't you even care about your own flesh and blood!?

OWEN: (*turns away from her*) I'd . . . just be in the way.

BESS: Nonsense! (*concerned*) Owen . . . what has gotten into you? You used to be so alive! But now, all you do is sit . . . Tell me what's the matter! Please?!

(*There is a long pause. Finally, OWEN slowly turns back to her.*)

OWEN: I ... I'm ... tired, Bess.

BESS: (*angry*) All right—just go on to bed, then!

(*She starts off, but he stops her.*)

OWEN: No! (*near tears*) I mean ... I'm <u>tired</u>! Of everything! My soul is sick ... and I'm <u>scared</u>, Bess—so very scared!

BESS: Scared of what?

OWEN: I look at myself, and I see that time has run out for me. I'm ... <u>old</u>. But, instead of the rock-solid faith I'm supposed to have ... I keep thinking, "What if it's not true? What if the things I've held dear and taught and latched onto all my life ... are all lies?" ... I'm not sure I <u>believe</u> in anything anymore, Bess ... and what's worse, I'm not sure I <u>want</u> to.

(*He turns away. BESS looks at him for a long moment, then sits, picks up a book from under the table, and begins reading.*)

BESS: Owen, we <u>have</u> to keep believing, especially when we may not want to. That's what believing in Jesus means ... to trust Him no matter what ... (*reads*) "Now on the first day of the week, Mary Magdalene and the other Mary came to see the tomb. And there was a great earthquake, for an angel of the Lord descended from heaven ... and the angel said to the women, '<u>Do not be afraid,</u> for I know that you seek Jesus, who was crucified. He is not here, for He is risen, as He said.' ... And as they went to tell His disciples, Jesus met them, saying, 'Rejoice! <u>Do not be afraid.</u>'"

OWEN: (*softly*) He is risen ... Do not be afraid.

BESS: (*she kneels beside him, holding his hands*) It's not lies, Owen. The fact that you're scared about not believing should tell you that ... I'm just as old as you are—just as near death. But I know that the same Jesus who has been with us all our lives—who is with us right now!—will be waiting for us on the other side of death with open arms ... you know that, too ... don't you?

OWEN: Yes.

BESS: Then there's no reason to be afraid.

(*A pause. OWEN looks at her, touches her cheek, and smiles.*)

OWEN: My lovely Bessie ... you always know what to say.

BESS: Sometimes we just have to go back to the basics.

OWEN: (*a deep breath*) What say we ... go take a peek at our new great-grandchild?

BESS: I was hoping you'd say that—I don't know how much more of this kneeling my knees can take!

(*He helps her up, then hugs her.*)

OWEN: Thank you, Bess.

BESS: You're welcome . . . now, c'mon!

(*They exit together, stage right. The lights fade on them. The spotlight hits the choir, who brings us **verse three** of the song.*)

CHOIR: And then one day I'll cross the river, I'll fight life's final war with pain;
And then as death gives way to victory, I'll see the lights of glory and I'll know He reigns!

(*At this point, the lights fade on the choir and a spot rises center-stage where LORI, in a chair, holds the newest member of the family. DAVE is beside her. After a few seconds, BOB and JOAN enter from stage left. They look very hopeful together. And after a few more seconds, OWEN and BESS enter from stage right. Everyone greets OWEN with a hug, and OWEN places his hand gently on the new baby's head. The entire family surrounds the chair in loving support of the child . . . And one another.*)

CHOIR: Because He lives, I can face tomorrow,
Because He lives, all fear is gone;
Because I know He holds the future,
And life is worth the living just because He lives.

(*Everyone, including the congregation, joins in.*)

ALL. Because He lives, I can face tomorrow,
Because He lives, all fear is gone;
Because I know He holds the future,
And life is worth the living just because He lives.

Christ the Lord Is Risen Today

TEXT: Charles Wesley
MUSIC: from *Lyra Davidica*, 1708

Charles Wesley is often regarded as history's greatest hymn writer. His hymns grew out of his awareness of a deeply personal relationship with Christ, and it is recorded that he wrote poems or hymns every day, resulting in over 6,500 hymns. He is recognized as a founder of the Methodist church, but his hymns are sung by all Christian churches.

"Christ the Lord Is Risen Today" is the definitive Easter hymn. It first appeared in 1739 entitled "Hymn for Easter Day," which is appropriate as most Christians are still singing it each Easter morning! It originally had eleven stanzas.

John Wesley, Charles's brother, included the text with the *Lyra Davidica* tune in his *Foundery Collection,* 1742. The Wesleys were important in introducing new types of tunes to hymnody, and they commented that there should be hymn tunes for "all sort and condition of men."

Christ the Lord is risen today, Alleluia!
Sons of men and angels say: Alleluia!
Raise your joys and triumphs high. Alleluia!
Sing, ye heav'ns, and earth reply: Alleluia!

Lives again our glorious King, Alleluia!
Where, O Death, is now thy sting? Alleluia!
Dying once He all doth save, Alleluia!
Where thy victory, O grave? Alleluia!

Love's redeeming work is done, Alleluia!
Fought the fight, the battle won, Alleluia!
Death in vain forbids Him rise, Alleluia!
Christ has opened Paradise, Alleluia!

Soar we now where Christ has led, Alleluia!
Foll'wing our exalted Head, Alleluia!
Made like Him, like Him we rise, Alleluia!
Ours the cross, the grave, the skies, Alleluia!

Christ the Lord Is Risen Today
A Dramatic Sketch
by
Deborah Craig-Claar

SYNOPSIS
Two brothers—Roman soldiers Antony and Cassius—have just been hired by a Jerusalem priest to perform a very special task: Spread the rumor that the garden tomb is empty because Jesus' disciples have stolen His body. But the brothers are not prepared for their first encounter—a woman named Mary who has quite a different version of the events. She leaves one brother converted, the other unconvinced. With great difficulty the brothers part, setting off on two different roads with two different stories. The events in this sketch are drawn from Matthew 28.

Performance Time: 6–7 minutes

WORSHIP USES
Easter Sunday; Pageants; General use

WORD MUSIC RESOURCES
- SATB Anthem, arr. by Bob Krogstad, #3010743165
  Choral Trax and Orchestration are available.
- SAB Anthem, arr. by Paul Johnson, #3010626169
  Choral Trax available

SETTING/PROPS
The scene can occur on an empty stage. A single Roman column might add some atmosphere. The only prop is a leather pouch of coins. Antony and Cassius should both wear some objects of Roman armor, including a helmet and sword.

CHARACTERS
CASSIUS, a young Roman soldier; zealous and stubborn, a man with a mission

ANTONY, Cassius's brother, also a soldier; although equally strong-willed, he is more introspective, and has been troubled of late

MARY, one of the young women at the tomb; she is filled with the awe and urgency of having just encountered the risen Christ

(ANTONY *enters, boldly striding center and stopping to look around. He appears irritated, anxious . . . and a bit preoccupied. He waits and paces for several more moments, his irritation growing. Finally,* CASSIUS *enters, almost on the run. He is full of zealous energy.*)

CASSIUS: (*as he enters*) Antony! Wait until you hear what I . . .

ANTONY: (*not hearing, cutting him off*) Where have you been?! Our guard assignment starts at dawn, Cassius, unless you've conveniently forgotten. It's practically midday. I've had to perform two jobs and still deal with the hysteria in this city.

CASSIUS: (*looking at him incredulously*) Pardon me, my dear brother, but the only hysteria in this city is yours. And since when have you been such a slave to the details of our assignments? Wasn't it yesterday that you said you were just about to believe in the Hebrews' stories of hell—and serving in Caesar's army was first-hand proof?

ANTONY: (*darkly*) Serving in Caesar's army hasn't improved one bit. I just don't like to waste time.

CASSIUS: What's been wrong with you lately? Ever since the beginning of the year you've been anxious, preoccupied, difficult; you haven't stayed at the garrison after watch to have a drink for months. In fact, you never seem to sit anymore, period. What are you looking for? What do you expect to happen?

ANTONY: (*gazing away*) I don't have any idea. If I knew, I wouldn't be waiting.

CASSIUS: Thirty years and I still don't have a clue as to what goes on in your stubborn head. For months you rush around as if something is going to happen any minute—and now these last three days, time can't seem to pass quickly enough for you.

ANTONY: Things are dark and filthy in this city. You can smell the stench in the air. I can't wait to move on.

CASSIUS: (*laughing sarcastically*) Still no stomach for executions, eh? What are you complaining about? You were nowhere near the hill of bones. This one was unusually short, anyway—Marcus told me it was over in less than three hours. Next time you'll draw crucifixion detail, then you'll wish you had been up there this time . . .

ANTONY: (*with great emotion, cutting him off*) Crucifixions are repugnant and barbaric, and those that discharge them are no better.

CASSIUS: Well aren't we being civilized?! Don't give me that. You've supervised dozens of crucifixions and have never so much as turned your head. What's so different about this one . . .

ANTONY: (*breaking him off again*) Nothing. Nothing at all. I just . . . (*he struggles for a moment, then retreats*) . . . never mind. I . . . haven't been feeling well. It's Jerusalem. I just need to . . . move on.

(*ANTONY turns, as if to exit.*)

CASSIUS: Well, this should improve the state of your health!

(*He throws a small pouch of coins to ANTONY, who catches it awkwardly.*)

ANTONY: What's this . . . ?

CASSIUS: Oh, just some incentive to stick around Jerusalem a little longer.

ANTONY: (*looking into the pouch*) Where did you get this?

CASSIUS: From a new colleague sworn to preserving the peace in the Roman Empire. (*pause*) His name is Annas.

ANTONY: (*dumbfounded*) Annas?! The Jews' Priest? Ciaphas's associate? He's always hated Rome.

CASSIUS: Well, unusual circumstances make unusual alliances. There's been a lot of turmoil over in the east garden since early this morning. One of the tombs there has been broken into and the body's disappeared.

(*ANTONY is more affected by this than one might expect.*)

ANTONY: (*quietly*) Disappeared?

CASSIUS: (*not noticing ANTONY'S reaction, going on*) So what's another grave robbing in a pit like Jerusalem? But unfortunately this was the grave of that fanatical Jewish prophet from Nazareth—the one whose excecution you found so distasteful.

ANTONY: (*too quickly*) I know the man you're speaking of. I've . . . been at several of His hillside gatherings . . . (*as an afterthought*) to watch for any signs of insurrection.

CASSIUS: Then maybe you've already heard. It seems He's been telling His followers that He would rise from the dead after three days. The absurdity of the claim wouldn't even be worth honoring with a rebuttal—but now there's been this very . . . awkward . . . coincidence of events. The third day and suddenly—no body. The last thing the Jewish leadership needs is a new surge of hysterical, miracle-claiming fanatics. (*pause*) Frankly, it's the last thing we need as well.

ANTONY: There's nothing we can do about an empty grave.

CASSIUS: Except explain it.

ANTONY: But we don't know what happened.

CASSIUS: What difference does that make? Someone took the body—it doesn't matter who. The priests want it blamed on Jesus' disciples. They're about as good a choice as anybody. (*smugly*) What a band of gullible simpletons.

ANTONY: Are you telling me we're being paid to spread a lie?

CASSIUS: We don't know if it's a lie! For all we know, it may be the truth. We're just . . . telling a story. Anyway, you tell a story enough times, it becomes the truth.

ANTONY: (*throwing money pouch back at CASSIUS*) I'm not going to accept money to spread a rumor!

(*A young woman, MARY, enters upstage. She is in a great hurry. She stops for a few moments to catch her breath, and bends down to adjust her sandal.*)

CASSIUS: The great moralist makes a stand. Well, have it your way. I'm sure this is one assignment I can handle on my own. (*he turns and sees MARY*) Here's someone now. Just watch. You may change your mind. (*he approaches MARY*) Pardon me, woman . . .

MARY: (*startled and moving away*) I was only fixing my sandal, sir, I'll be going quickly . . .

CASSIUS: No, you don't understand. You've done nothing wrong. I . . . just want to speak with you for a few moments.

MARY: Oh. (*struggling*) Please, I'm really in a great hurry . . .

CASSIUS: Where are you headed?

MARY: Into the city. I . . . have important news to tell some people there. Then, we're to go to Galilee.

CASSIUS: What a coincidence. I have news too. Let me tell you mine, then you can take it with you and tell it to your friends in the city, and in Galilee.

MARY: (*uncomfortable*) I truly thank you, but . . .

CASSIUS: (*continuing hastily*) Wait until you've heard what's happened over in the east garden, to one of the tombs . . .

MARY: (*suddenly highly interested*) Why I've just come from there . . .

ANTONY: (*now joining them*) You have?!

MARY: (*to CASSIUS*) What have you heard?

CASSIUS: (*a bit thrown off guard, but continuing*) Well there is a tomb there with a body missing . . .

MARY: Yes, yes, that's true! The tomb is empty!

ANTONY: You <u>saw</u> it . . .?!

MARY: I walked inside it!

CASSIUS: You know, of course, whose tomb it was—that carpenter from Nazareth who was killed for crimes against the Jews . . .

MARY: Jesus of Nazareth . . .

CASSIUS: Yes. And you should also know that it was His disciples who stole the body, probably to perpetuate His outrageous prediction about Himself.

MARY: No, no. That's not true. His disciples were nowhere near the tomb last night Besides, the tomb is empty because Jesus Christ is alive.

(*ANTONY reacts strongly to this news. CASSIUS remains sarcastic.*)

CASSIUS: Oh, is He?

MARY: He's risen from the dead.

CASSIUS: And how do you know that?

MARY: The angel told us so . . .

CASSIUS: (*laughing*) Oh, the <u>angel</u> told you. Well, this certainly is a day for telling stories.

MARY: (*with quiet conviction*) . . . and then we saw Jesus ourselves.

(*CASSIUS stops abruptly and just stares at MARY. ANTONY excitedly moves to her.*)

ANTONY: (*urgently*) Tell me about it.

MARY: It was as if we were looking into the sun, but could see clearly. I've never seen so clearly before. He walked up and greeted us, and we fell at His feet and worshipped Him. He told us to run and tell His followers He'd be going before us, into Galilee. He told us He'd see us again in Galilee.

(*CASSIUS has been fuming the entire time, and now comes storming forward*)

CASSIUS: This is lunacy . . . !

ANTONY: (*turning to CASSIUS directly, suddenly taking the offensive*) And how do you think the grave was broken into, Cassius? That tomb was <u>sealed</u>...

CASSIUS: (*stammering angrily*) A band of men <u>could</u> have moved the stone...

ANTONY: How did they get to it? The tomb was guarded, constantly.

CASSIUS: Octavius and Lucius. They were probably drunk and slept through the whole thing...

ANTONY: So who did she see, Cassius? Who?

CASSIUS: You're becoming as deluded as she is!! (*turning to MARY, tensely*) I'm sorry, but we obviously have two different versions of the events. Thank you for the information. Good day.

(*ANTONY and MARY look at each other for a moment.*)

MARY: Yes, I... have many people to see. (*looking at ANTONY*) Many people. God be with you.

(*MARY turns and quickly exits. ANTONY stares after her for a moment then looks at the ground. CASSIUS, grumbling, angrily paces, and is oblivious to his brother's emotions.*)

CASSIUS: Well, if that isn't typical of the derangement that's enveloped this city. Not only are people believing this fabrication about the Nazarene, now they're seeing Him as well. I think you're right—this city is dark and filthy. Well come on, this job will be easier nearer the center of town. The people are wealthier and more discerning there, and will accept a more logical explanation of the circumstance... (*begins to be distracted as he sees something in the distance*) Look... there are three men coming this way.

(*CASSIUS moves to exit, then looks back. ANTONY is taking off his helmet and sword, and laying them on the ground.*)

CASSIUS: Antony, hurry... we've already wasted too much time and... (*pauses, stunned, watching ANTONY for a moment*) What are you doing?

ANTONY: Moving on.

CASSIUS: What?

ANTONY: I'm going to Galilee.

CASSIUS: What are you talking about? Our assignment in Jerusalem doesn't end for another fortnight.

ANTONY: You don't understand. I'm not just leaving Jerusalem. I'm ... (*drawing in his breath for a moment, then—*) ... leaving Rome.

CASSIUS: You can't be serious. (*pause, ANTONY continues to work*) You <u>are</u> deluded. What do you think you're going to do?

ANTONY: First I'm going to see an empty tomb. Then I'm going to go to Galilee. And after that ... after that I think I'll know. (*he looks down for a moment, then up to look CASSIUS directly in the eyes*) I wish you'd come, too. Just ... to find out what really happened.

CASSIUS: (*still angry, and now hurt*) I know what really happened. I'm being paid to tell people about it, remember?

(*ANTONY nods, and looks at his brother with deep sadness.*)

ANTONY: I'll miss you. (*a long pause—no reply*) Cassius. Please ... come find Him.

CASSIUS: (*coldly, not looking at ANTONY*) I'm sorry. I'm busy. I ... have a story to tell.

(*CASSIUS turns and exits.*)

ANTONY: (*pause, then quietly, almost to himself*) So do I.

(*ANTONY turns and exits the other direction, leaving his helmet and sword on the ground. If the hymn is being played or sung, the music should begin as ANTONY exits and should continue without a break as one continuous worship event.*)

Go to Dark Gethsemane

TEXT: James Montgomery
MUSIC: Richard Redhead

British hymn writer James Montgomery described himself as a "lay" hymn writer, and contributed many hymns that are still in use today, including "Prayer Is the Soul's Sincere Desire," "Angels from the Realms of Glory," and "Stand Up and Bless the Lord." A journalist by trade, Montgomery's texts have both the evangelicalism of the Wesleyan movement, and the literary merit of Watts. Thus, they are still meaningful and useful today.

Go to dark Gethsemane,
You that feel the tempter's pow'r;
Your Redeemer's conflict see,
Watch with Him one bitter hour:
Turn not from His griefs away—
Learn of Jesus Christ to pray.

Follow to the judgment hall,
View the Lord of life arraigned;
O the wormwood and the gall!
O the pangs His soul sustained!
Shun not suff'ring, shame or loss—
Learn of Him to bear the cross.

Calv'ry's mournful mountain climb;
There, adoring at His feet,
Mark the miracle of time,
God's own sacrifice complete:
"It is finished!" hear Him cry—
Learn of Jesus Christ to die.

Go to Dark Gethsemane

A Dramatic Sketch
by
Deborah Craig-Claar

SYNOPSIS
In four short monologues, the disciple John traces his personal spiritiual journey from the fateful night in Gethsemane, to Pilate's courtyard, to the foot of the cross on Golgotha, and finally to the empty garden tomb. In addition to being performed as a single monologue, the piece can also fit within the congregational singing of the hymn, or be used as a sequence of short dramatic scenes throughout a single service.

| Performance Time: | 5-7 minutes with hymn |

WORSHIP USES
Easter season; Palm Sunday, Good Friday, Easter uses

WORD MUSIC RESOURCES
- "Why Do You Seek the Living among the Dead?"
  SATB Anthem, Written & Arranged by Robert Sterling, #3010749163
  Choral Trax and Orchestration are available.

SETTING/PROPS
The scene is scripted to occur on an empty stage. There are no props. Because the scene is Biblical, John should be costumed accordingly.

CHARACTERS
JOHN–   the disciple, reflecting on his weaknesses, empowered by Christ's strength.

(JOHN is either discovered by light centerstage, or slowy enters to stand center stage. He looks up at the audience for a few moments, then speaks--simply, with quiet emotion.)

JOHN: Questions. For three years, almost every day, Jesus had asked us questions. "Who do you say that I am?" "Are you not worth more to God than the birds of the air?" (*quietly*) "Oh you of little faith . . . why do you still doubt?" I rarely had the answer. But that had never stopped my voice before. I made foolish promises, I asked foolish questions . . . but I spoke. That's why I couldn't understand what happened that night.

(*JOHN moves to another area of the stage.*)

It was such a simple question this time: "Will you stay with Me one hour?" He asked. "John, will you watch with Me and pray?" With one breath I vowed steadfastness—and with the next breath I retreated into the sanctuary of sleep. The flesh made promises, but the spirit turned and ran. Three times He asked, three times I slept—until . . . I was awakened by torches, angry shouting. . .and another quiet question: "Are you betraying the Son of Man with a kiss?" I could only watch helplessly as my friend became a traitor, my Master became a prisoner. . . and as I became a coward.

(*JOHN moves to another area of the stage; either the choir or soloist can sing the first stanza of the hymn, Scripture can be inserted, or the monologue can continue without break.*)

The next morning I found myself standing in a crowded, dirty courtyard. People shoved and pushed one another, children cried. I stood on the edge, staring at the ground, hoping no one would recognize me. Then suddenly, the roar stopped. The people around me pointed toward two men standing on a balcony. I was staring into the sun and still couldn't see them clearly. I could only hear the voice: "Who do you want me to release to you?" it said, and then, "What shall I do with Jesus who is called the Christ?" (*pause*) Simple questions. Just like the night before. And just like the night before, my answer was silence. The crowd yelled "Give us Barabbas," then they yelled "Crucify Him!" and then they led my Lord away to His death . . . leaving me to mine.

(*JOHN moves again; either the choir or soloists can sing the second stanza of the hymn, more Scripture can be inserted, or the monologue can continue without break.*)

I'm not sure how I climbed the hill that afternoon. The sky was so black, at times I couldn't find my way. At first I was sure I was cutting my feet on the sharp rocks, but later I realized it was shattered bones. I probably would have turned back if I hadn't found His mother, huddled at His feet, silently crying. I knelt beside her, weeping as well. Then, all became silent, and a last question was offered to the indifferent heavens: "My God, why have You forsaken Me?" The answer was a rush of cold wind, and the cry of a last breath. And then the world joined me in my silence.

(*JOHN moves again; the choir or soloist can sing the third stanza of the hymn, more Scripture can be inserted, or the monologue can continue without break.*)

Death is such an indelible thing. Continuous. . . unremitting. It's made of unmovable stones and perfect darkness. And it offers a final answer, because it stops all questions. Forever. That's why I couldn't believe the women that third morning. Stones that had moved, darkness turned to day. . .?! I must have run to the tomb with Peter just to prove to myself that the world was still the way it had been created—where death has the final word. But when I got there, I knew immediately that everything had been changed—for eternity. I saw the empty tomb with my own eyes; I held His burial cloths in my own hands. Then Mary told me the question the angel had asked: "Why do you seek the living among the dead?"

(*Introduction music to the final musical sequence, used as an underscore, can begin here.*)

And suddenly I understood—my hesitations, my silences. I'd always come to Jesus with my fears, looking for Him among my old habits, my old excuses and doubts. But they were dead now. All that was put behind me that morning at the tomb. My old self was dead, as surely as the stone and clay. And now Jesus Christ—the answer to every question, alive and lifted high—was reaching back to us, showing us a way out of the grave, lifting us to rise with Him!

(*The choir or soloist may sing the last stanza of the hymn, or the entire hymn can be sung, or another Easter resurrection anthem may be sung. Word's Easter anthem "Why Do You Seek the Living among The Dead?" would be a particularly appropriate choice.*)

In the Garden

TEXT and MUSIC: C. Austin Miles

The writer of this favorite hymn gave this account (Sanville's *Forty Gospel Hymn Stories*):

One day in March 1912, I was seated in the darkroom, where I kept my photographic equipment and organ. I drew my Bible toward me; it opened at my favorite chapter, John 20. That meeting of Jesus and Mary had lost none of its power to charm.

As I read it that day, I seemed to be part of the scene. I became a silent witness to that dramatic moment in Mary's life, when she knelt before her Lord, and cried, "Rabonni!"

My hands were resting on the Bible while I stared at the light blue wall. As the light faded I seemed to be standing at the entrance of a garden, looking down a gently winding path, shaded by olive branches. A woman in white, with head bowed, hand clasping her throat, as if to choke back her sobs, walked slowly into the shadows. It was Mary. As she came to the tomb, upon which she placed her hand, she bent over to look in, and hurried away.

John, in flowing robe, appeared, looking at the tomb; then came Peter, who entered the tomb, followed slowly by John.

As they departed, Mary reappeared, leaning her head upon her arm at the tomb, she wept. Turning herself, she saw Jesus standing, so did I. I knew it was He. She knelt before Him, with arms outstretched, and looking into His face cried, "Rabboni!"

I awakened in full light, gripping the Bible, with muscles tense and nerves vibrating. Under the inspiration of this vision I wrote as quickly as the words would be formed. The poem was exactly as it has since appeared. That same evening I wrote the music.

I come to the garden alone,
While the dew is still on the roses;
And the voice I hear, falling on my ear,
The Son of God discloses.

REFRAIN:
And He walks with me, and He talks with me,
And He tells me I am His own;
And the joy we share as we tarry there
None other has ever known.

He speaks, and the sound of His voice
Is so sweet the birds hush their singing;
And the melody that He gave to me
Within my heart is ringing.

I'd stay in the garden with Him
Tho the night around me be falling;
But He bids me go—thru the voice of woe,
His voice to me is calling.

In the Garden
A Dramatic Sketch
by
Deborah Craig-Claar

SYNOPSIS
Pearle is a caustic but endearing senior citizen who has found "home" (and a place of worship) in a flower garden which she faithfully tends in a city park. At sunrise on Easter morning, she defends her flowers against a barage of intruders, finally meeting a fellow octagenarian, Herb, a lonely, grumpy man who has wandered away from a sunrise Easter service in the park. As they battle and banter their way to an understanding, they discover a mutual loneliness and essential Easter truths revealed in God's created world.

| Performance Time: | 5-7 minutes |

WORSHIP USES
Easter season; Resurrection themes

WORD MUSIC RESOURCES
- Studio Series Artist Trax, as recorded by Sandi Patti, #3017766209

SETTING/PROPS
The scene takes place in a city park at sunrise. A single bench and trash can are centerstage. There should be a few pieces of trash scattered about. The flower garden that Pearle is working with is imagined as being just beyond the front of the stage. Props include a rake, a large tray with a dozen containers of bedding flowers, and a large basket of gardening tools including canvas working gloves, a spade, and a spray can of Black Flag insect spray.

CHARACTERS
PEARLE, about 80, she still does and thinks everything she did at 30, only a bit slower; she's fiesty, stubborn, but very caring.

HERB, also about 80, a man who has seen a lot of life and at the moment is feeling its weight; he walks with a cane and talks with a grumble.

MEL, a policeman—with a nightstick

TODD, a park sanitation engineer—with a pointed stick and bag

SHELLY, a jogger—with a sweatband

(*The scene opens on an empty set. A tape of birds chirping to help set the time is helpful, but not mandatory. Suddenly PEARLE runs on from stage R, as if she is late for an appointment, and stops C stage. She carries a large tray with small bedding containers of flowers. She puts them down, groans, turns and exits R, returning a few moments later with a large basket of gardening tools, including a rake under her arm. She sets them down, slowly kneels, and puts on her work gloves. But just before she starts, she stops, feels around on her head, wrinkles her face in exasperation and exclaims—*)

PEARLE: Finch feathers!!

(*MEL enters from stage R, holding a wide-brimmed straw sun hat*)

MEL: Top o' the mornin' to ya, Miss Patterson. I found this at the park entrance. I knew it couldn't belong to anyone else.

PEARLE: (*more put out than relieved*) Thank you, Officer O'Reily.

MEL: 'Course you won't be needin' it for a couple more hours. The sun's just barely up.

PEARLE: Thank you, Officer. . .

MEL: Officer?! Now how long have we known each other? How many years have you been comin' to work on your little garden here in Westside Park? Three years? Four?

PEARLE: (*through clenched teeth*) Seven. . . (*She looks at him; he's waiting expectantly; she manages—*) . . . Mel.

MEL: (*walks away a few steps, twirling the hat on his finger*) Startin' a little early this morning, aren't you, Pearle? I mean, compared to most other Sundays?

PEARLE: Actually, I'm a little late. . .

MEL: (*very patronizing*) Bet'cha I know what's happened. You got addled, which is more'n understandable, considerin' yer age n'all. Yep, you've got your April Sundays mixed up—and you "sprang forward" two weeks early! And that always makes you one hour late. (*PEARLE looks at him incredulously; he begins to get confused*) Wait a minute. That would mean "falling-back" makes you one hour early. (*scratching his head with his nightstick*) Now how can that be?

PEARLE: (*out of patience*) Officer O'Reily, I know what month it is, what Sunday it is, and what hour it is!

MEL: (*right behind her, speaking in an exaggerated tone as if to a child*) Of course you do! That's why you're busy digging in your garden—just like a little bunny! (*He places the sun hat on her head firmly, causing it to go down over her eyes*) Happy Easter, Pearle!

47

(*MEL gives her a playful tap on the head with his nightstick, then strolls offstage, whistling some appropriate Easter ditty. PEARLE angrily flips up her brim, muttering to herself.*)

PEARLE: _____'s finest. (*fill in your own town*) No wonder law and order is in such trouble in this country. (*returns to her tools*) And why does everyone always feel the need to tap me with their sticks? My internist taps my knees, my dentist depresses my tongue, the kid down the block slaps me with his hockey stick . . .

(*She starts unpacking the plants. TODD enters behind her, humming the same Easter ditty as MEL. He is picking up trash with a long pointed stick and depositing it in a bag slung over his shoulder. He spears a packet of seeds and holds it up, examining it.*)

TODD: What in the world is that?

PEARLE: Hey, put those back. Those are zinnias!

TODD: (*still examining it*) They look like seeds to me.

PEARLE: (*aiming her spade at him*) Drop 'em, mister!

TODD: (*good naturedly*) Yes M'am . . . (*He tosses the packet to PEARLE, who, more determined than ever, goes back to her plants, mumbling all the while, just as SHELLY jogs on. She pauses, jogging in place, smiles, looks at PEARLE and her "garden," then starts to speak.*)

SHELLY: (*tapping PEARLE on the shoulder*) Excuse me. Happy Easter! What a beautiful garden you've . . .

PEARLE: (*bellowing*) Don't tap me, don't touch me, don't breathe on me! (*Shelly, startled, backs up*) And don't jog on those hyacinths! Off! Out!

(*SHELLY quickly jogs out as PEARLE resumes working, muttering to herself more angrily than ever.*)

PEARLE: Crazy aerobic adolescents. They're more dangerous to gardens than locusts.

(*HERB enters, moving slowly to the bench with a cane. PEARLE continues to work, oblivious. HERB sits, watching PEARLE for a moment, then yells—*)

HERB: What're you doing in the dirt, old woman?!

(*PEARLE, startled, yells back.*)

PEARLE: You don't have to yell—I'm not hard of hearing!

HERB: Well I am. And if I don't yell, I can't hear what I'm saying! (*He waits a moment, as PEARLE continues to work. Then he yells again, poking her in the back with his cane.*) I said, what're you doing in the dirt?!

PEARLE: (*springing to her feet, grabbing her rake*) That's enough! Aaaiiee.... (*Raising her rake, she charges at him, as he raises his cane and they begin to spar.*)

HERB: Help! Park mugging! Someone get their video camera!

(*There is a whistle offstage and MEL comes running on.*)

MEL: All right, freeze! Police! Throw your weapons on the ground!

(*HERB spins around to face MEL*)

HERB: Officer, I can assure you that it is I who was assaulted by this... this... felon. Assaulted, attacked, and... and... sexually harassed.

(*PEARLE drops her rake and stares at HERB, aghast.*)

MEL: Sir, you have my sympathy.
(*He grabs his cane and rake*)
I'll just hold onto these... weapons... as evidence.
(*As he leaves, under his breath to HERB*)
Pick 'em up on your way out the front gate. (*beat*) Good luck.

(*MEL exits. HERB & PEARLE look at each other angrily. Then HERB sits on the bench and PEARLE kneels by her flowers again.*)

HERB: Well, that's just fine. Great. How am I gonna walk?

PEARLE: How am I gonna plant?

HERB: One can hardly be compared to the other.

PEARLE: That's true. At least I'm adding beauty to the earth.

(*HERB grunts. There are a few more moments of cold silence, then HERB leans forward, looking more closely.*)

HERB: What is it that you're doing? Are you on the park department's swing shift?

PEARLE: (*continuing to work, not looking up*) No, no, this is my garden. I just... borrow the park.

HERB: Have they ever asked for it back?

PEARLE: Not in the seven years I've been planting.

HERB: I'd think they'd have laws about things like this. Or at least an ordinance. How come you aren't planting flowers at home?

PEARLE: I haven't got a home, exactly.

HERB: Neither have I.

PEARLE: (*suddenly jumping up*) I knew it! You're a vagrant! A bag . . . gentleman. Don't move—(*she grabs a black spray can out of her basket*)—I've got mace!!

HERB: (*cowering*) That's Black Flag!!

PEARLE: (*aiming*) Even better.

HERB: You crazy woman, what I meant is that I don't <u>own</u> my own home anymore. I live in a retirement village.

PEARLE: (*putting can down and returning to her task*) Oh. Well, so do I. (*she decides to spray some of her plants*)

HERB: You do? Which one?

PEARLE: Rock Haven.

HERB: That's impossible. That's where I live.

PEARLE: No, you don't. I've never seen you there.

HERB: How could you? You're always out here, playing in the dirt and annoying pedestrians.

PEARLE: OK. Prove you live at Rock Haven. (*quickly*) What's the orderly's name?

HERB: Raoul.

PEARLE: What color's the carpet in the lounge?

HERB: Green.

PEARLE: What do they serve on Tuesdays?

HERB: Meatloaf.

PEARLE: Ah hah! I knew you were an imposter. (*back to work*) It's salisbury steak.

HERB: No, it's meatloaf, <u>but</u> . . . I will grant you that it's impossible to tell the difference.

(*PEARLE starts to laugh—stops herself—but cannot hide a smile. Her tone softens a bit, as she continues to work.*)

PEARLE: Well if you're a Rock Haven inmate, what are you doing, . . .?

(*She looks at him expectantly for his name*)

HERB: Herb.

PEARLE: Herb. What are you doing out here, Herb, at (*looks at watch*) 6:48 in the morning?

HERB: I'm not here by choice. See that group of people shivering up on the knoll over by the baseball field? That's the sunrise service from my son and daughter-in-law's church. I escaped during the Lord's Prayer.

PEARLE: Won't they worry?

HERB: They don't even know I'm gone. See how they're all squinting? They can't see a thing. Pastor Bob never did have enough sense to turn everybody away from the rising sun.

PEARLE: Some people go to great lengths to celebrate Easter.

HERB: Well, I think I'm better off not celebrating it. I never was much of a morning person. Easter's for preachers and kids.

PEARLE: Well, if that isn't the sorriest attitude I've ever heard. Frankly, you haven't got much choice about celebrating Easter—not when the world's doing it for you.

HERB: What are you talking about?

PEARLE: (*getting up and sitting next to HERB, a plant bed in her hand*) Now surely you don't think Easter and spring happening at the same time is a coincidence, do you? Everywhere you look something is budding or opening or stretching. If it has a root and a stem, then it's telling you the Easter story.

HERB: (*interested, but suspicious*) Is that a fact.

PEARLE: Absolutely. (*holds up the plant in her hand*) See this soil? That's all the tomb was made of—rock and soil and clay. But just as stones and death couldn't hold the Lord, so each plant breaks through the soil and climbs toward the sky. Life—rising, again and again.

(*She gazes at the flower, smiling; then, abruptly, she hands the plant to HERB*)

Happy Easter.

(*PEARLE leans forward, rumaging in her basket. HERB stares at the plant for a moment. When he speaks, his tone has also softened.*)

HERB: So this is where you always come Easter Sunday?

PEARLE: This is where I always come <u>every</u> Sunday. Oh, I go to services around eleven, mind you, but here's where I . . . worship. I don't have much family left, and after I gave up my house and moved to Rock Haven, little by little this became home. I find I don't think as much about growing old when I'm here—I don't feel as sorry for myself, I don't feel as alone. And I'm surrounded by Easter, all year. That big tree right there keeps me near the cross, and my flowers keep me near the risen Lord.

(*A pause. PEARLE turns and looks at HERB, who has been very thoughtful.*)

Do you have a church to go to?

HERB: I haven't been in a church since my wife Ellen died five years ago.

PEARLE: Oh. (*She smiles tenderly at him for a moment, then speaks with her former energy*) Well, you can come with me from now on.

HERB: What?

PEARLE: You heard me. Meet me at the east door at 7:00. This sunrise business is only on special occasions.

HERB: Now wait just a minute, I . . .

PEARLE: (*cutting him off*) I know, I know. You're not a morning person. Well, maybe that's what's ailin' ya, Herb. You need to become one. You know, Pastor Bob knew <u>exactly</u> what he was doing when he had everyone face the rising sun.

HERB: (*squinting into the horizon*) Uh oh. Look at that woman in the lavender hat running around on top of the knoll like a dog chasin' its tail . . . and that man in a tree with the binoculars. I guess the sun's out of their eyes now and my son's realized I'm gone.

PEARLE: (*also looking*) Looks like the service is over. I'm sorry you missed the sermon.

HERB: Nah. I didn't miss a thing. You and this garden were a pretty strong sermon, if you ask me. (*HERB stands and then offers his hand to PEARLE.*) C'mon. It's time for church.

(*HERB and PEARLE begin to exit the stage together as the musical introduction for "In the Garden" begins.*)

Let us Break Bread Together

TEXT and MUSIC:
Traditional Spiritual

This African-American spiritual is of unknown origins. Although traditionally thought of as a communion song, there are scholars who feel that African slaves may have used the tune as a "gathering" song to convene secret meetings of African-Americans that were prohibited by law during the Civil War period. Whatever the case, the song is today used as a song for communion.

> Let us break bread together on our knees;
> Let us break bread together on our knees;
> When I fall on my knees with my face to the rising sun,
> O Lord, have mercy on me.
>
> Let us drink the cup together on our knees;
> Let us drink the cup together on our knees;
> When I fall on my knees with my face to the rising sun,
> O Lord, have mercy on me.
>
> Let us praise God together on our knees;
> Let us praise God together on our knees;
> When I fall on my knees with my face to the rising sun,
> O Lord, have mercy on me.

Let Us Break Bread Together
A Dramatic Sketch
by Phil Lollar

SYNOPSIS
Just prior to the Lord's Supper, a family reflects on their lives and relationships with each other.

| Performance Time: | 7-10 minutes with communion. |

WORSHIP USES
Any service where communion is observed.

SETTING/PROPS
A worship service. No special technical requirements.

CHARACTERS
FATHER-   40s
MOTHER-   40s
SON or DAUGHTER- teenager

PASTOR
CHOIR or ENSEMBLE

(*The lights are down. Out of the darkness, the disembodied voice of the pastor is heard.*)

PASTOR: Before we partake of the Lord's Supper, let's take a few moments to truly examine ourselves and reflect on our lives and our relationships during the past few weeks.

(*Lights rise to reveal a family scattered around the stage: father, mother, son/daughter [the part could be either]. The parents are in their mid-40s and the kid is a teen. They all look like they hate each other. What we hear are their thoughts. MOM and DAD freeze as the SON/DAUGHTER start us off.*)

SON/
DAUGHTER: "Examine ourselves?" Ha! It's not *me* who needs examining—it's my parents. They're crazy! Mom still thinks I'm four years old—always trying to make me wear clothes I don't want to wear and do things I don't want to do . . . She never talks <u>to</u> me, she talks <u>at</u> me . . . And she <u>never</u> listens . . . Neither does my Dad. Sometimes, I'll talk right to him, and he just stares into space. It's like, "Earth to Dad! Earth to Dad!" And when he <u>does</u> listen, he goes from being Zombie-man to Frankenstein. Like yesterday, I asked him if he would take me to the mall, and he said: "Why do you want to go to the mall so much for? Don't you like staying home?" Staying home? Like that's my idea of a <u>real</u> great time   . . . Besides, I knew what he <u>really</u> meant—"Why are you hanging around with all those friends we don't like?". . .

I think he gets a lot of satisfaction out of cutting them down . . . They never let me do <u>anything</u> I want to do. They think I'm gonna get into some sort of trouble or something . . . <u>That's</u> the <u>real</u> problem—they don't trust me! Why can't they see that it's <u>my</u> life!?

(*HE/SHE freezes, and MOTHER unfreezes.*)

MOTHER: "Reflect on our lives?" I don't <u>have</u> a life. I have an unruly teenager and an absent husband . . . I really don't know what I'm going to do with that child . . . I guess I shouldn't be surprised—he/she has never listened. He/She has always been stubborn, ever since he/she was a little boy/girl . . . I know independence is important—but so is obedience . . . (*she motions to the father*) Of course, <u>he's</u> no help at all. He's always working late at the office, or gone on some business trip. And even when he's <u>here</u>, he might as well <u>not</u> be. I ask him a question and get a one-word answer or a grunt for a response . . . Maybe he's having an affair . . . All the experts on the talk shows say working late, lots of business trips and always being tired are sure signs. Of course, they also said that men having affairs usually compliment their wives to hide a guilty conscience . . . He hasn't complimented me in 10 years . . . (*sighs*) Some family . . . why can't they see things my way?

(*She freezes, and the FATHER unfreezes.*)

FATHER: "Relationships," huh? . . . I don't think I have any . . . after that mall incident the other day, my son/daughter has disowned me . . . and I haven't had the energy to talk to my wife in months . . . In fact, I haven't had the inclination to talk to either of them . . . I've been so tired! Working my tail off—extra hours, long sales trips . . . I can't help it if I have to work late. I'm in the middle of a huge project! . . . I know they'd love it if I could be home every night— so would I! But that's just not the way it is! . . . I have a *job*—a job that helps keep us in our house and driving our cars and eating good food . . . I know it's hard, but there's nothing I can do about it right now—not if we want security and a good life and solid future! That's all I'm trying to do here! . . . I'm under so much pressure! Why can't they *see* that?!

(*He freezes, and the PASTOR now enters and speaks.*)

PASTOR: And the people followed Him, for they had never seen His like before. Wherever He went, crowds waited to see the Man who had performed such wondrous miracles and spoken such wonderful words of life. "Blessed are the merciful, for they shall receive mercy . . . Blessed are the peacemakers, for they shall be called the sons of God . . . Love your enemies and pray for those who persecute you . . . Do not lay up for yourselves treasures on earth, but lay up for yourselves treasures in heaven—for where your treasure is, there will your heart be also . . .

Seek first the Kingdom of God, and His righteousness; and all these things shall be added to you . . . Judge not, lest you be judged . . . Do unto others as you would have them do unto you . . . Love one another." Many know of these words: the words of life. They have heard them again and again—dozens of times . . . And yet, somehow, they never really <u>listen</u> to them . . . It was the same with those of His time—people who heard, but did not listen . . . even among His closest followers there were those who did not understand His full purpose . . . why He came . . . and why He died . . . At their last supper together, He told them of what was to come, and asked them to eat and drink in remembrance of Him . . . And He asks that of us today—to examine ourselves before we eat of the bread and drink of the cup, and if we have something against our brother or sister, to leave our gift at the altar and first be reconciled to our brother or sister, and then partake. For in doing so, we proclaim His death until He comes . . .

(The choir now begins humming "Let Us Break Bread Together." The family realizes that they haven't been remembering Christ, but have been wallowing in self. They look at one another, then slowly move to centerstage, just in front of the communion table. There they hug each other, then kneel before the Lord's Supper. The PASTOR once again speaks.)

PASTOR: "Whoever eats this bread and drinks this cup of the Lord in an unworthy manner will be guilty of the body and blood of the Lord . . . for he eats and drinks judgment to himself, not discerning the Lord's body . . ." Let us reconcile ourselves to each other, and then, if you are able, come kneel with us in front of the altar as we partake of the Lord's Supper.

(The lights rise full on the auditorium. The choir keeps humming for a few minutes to give people a chance to move to each other. Then, as the choir director deems prudent, the choir sings the first verse of "Let Us Break Bread Together," while the pastor and the servers prepare the bread.)

SINGERS: Let us break bread together on our knees;
Let us break bread together on our knees;
When I fall on my knees, with my face to the rising sun,
O Lord, have mercy on me.

PASTOR: "And on the night in which He was betrayed, Jesus took the bread, blessed and broke it, and gave it to the disciples saying, 'Take, eat; for this is My body.'"

(*The bread is consumed. The choir then sings the second verse of "Let Us Break Bread Together," while the PASTOR and the servers prepare the juice.*)

SINGERS: Let us drink the cup together on our knees;
Let us drink the cup together on our knees;
When I fall on my knees, with my face to the rising sun,
O Lord, have mercy on me.

PASTOR: "Jesus then took the bread, blessed it and gave it to them saying, 'Drink from it, all of you. For this is My blood of the new covenant, which is shed for many for the remission of sins.'"

(*The wine is consumed. The PASTOR speaks again.*)

PASTOR: "For as often as you do this, do it in remembrance of me." Let's rejoice together!

(*The choir/congregation then sings the final verse of "Let Us Break Bread Together."*)

SINGERS: Let us praise God together on our knees;
Let us praise God together on our knees;
When I fall on my knees, with my face to the rising sun,
O Lord, have mercy on me!

Oh, How He Loves You and Me

TEXT and MUSIC: Kurt Kaiser
© Copyright 1975 WORD MUSIC (a div. of WORD RECORDS and MUSIC) All Rights Reserved. International Copyright Secured.

When asked to detail the story of this now-standard worship chorus, Kurt Kaiser commented:

"There really is no 'spectacular story,' as such. Down through the years, I've had the habit of jotting down brief little thoughts on a napkin or manuscript paper. I had written the line, "Oh, how He loves you and me" in the top corner of some manuscript paper, and one day decided to finish it. It all came out in about ten minutes. The person who really brought the song to life was the gospel artist Evie Tornquist. I recommended she record it in a medley with the hymn, "Jesus Loves Me." She did, and it really caught on after that. It has been printed and recorded thousands of times. People tell me all the time how meaningful the song is to them. I'm always humbled, moved, and grateful to God for that."

> Oh, how He loves you and me.
> Oh, how He loves you and me.
> He gave His life, what more could He give?
> Oh, how He loves you;
> Oh, how He loves me;
> Oh, how He loves you and me!
>
> Jesus to Calv'ry did go,
> His love for mankind to show;
> What He did there brought hope from despair:
> Oh, how He loves you;
> Oh, how He loves me;
> Oh, how He loves you and me!

Oh, How He Loves You and Me
A Dramatic Sketch
by
Deborah Craig-Claar

SYNOPSIS
It is the annual Sunday School Easter Egg Hunt on the church's front lawn (always held during the "big 11:00 service") and plucky Miss Yackanelli is valiantly managing the festivities. Everyone is having a wonderful time except too-cool Taylor, whose rejection of the eggs . . . and Easter itself . . . prompts a tender conversation, and a simpler, deeper look at the day. In addition to being used for worship services, this short, gently humorous sketch is also well-suited for Sunday school and children's programs.

| Performance Time: | 5-7 minutes with hymn |

WORSHIP USES
Easter; Sunday school; Children's programs; Services about God's love

WORD MUSIC RESOURCES
- SATB Anthem, by Kurt Kaiser, #3010037163
- Orchestra arr., Sunday Sounds Series, arr. by Ken Barker, #3015051253

SETTING/PROPS
The scene occurs on a large church lawn, so there is no set per se. There should be several lawn chairs centerstage and a very durable cooler. (An adult will need to stand on it.) Miss Yackanelli carries a large wicker basket with at least two chocolate bunnies, dyed eggs (real), jelly beans and some marshmallow chicks. She also carries (and uses) a bull horn. (The bull horn is a fun addition, but isn't mandatory.) Taylor has a Gameboy pocket video game.

CHARACTERS
MISS YACKANELLI, 40 something, a dedicated and tireless Sunday school director; she fluctuates between high energy directives and tender sharing.

TAYLOR BRADLEY, 8-10 (can be played by either gender); precocious and glib (without appearing rude or disrespectful), "too cool" and "too wise" for bunnies and eggs, but with a chink in his armor of hipness which allows in another aspect of Easter.

(*As the scene begins, MISS YACKANELLI enters at full voltage, bull horn activated. Consider having her enter through the audience. There is first a loud whistle blast, then she enters. Whenever she speaks to the children, it is in that exaggerated "I'm speaking-to-children" voice. There should be a high degree of contrast between this voice and her regular voice.*)

MISS YACKANELLI: It's 11:00, let's move it on out to the front lawn!! I should be seeing lots of little legs and little bodies moving ... I'm not seeing enough legs and bodies moving ...

(*She turns around and her sudden change of expression tells the story.*)

No, no, wait, too many legs and bodies ... not so fast! Slow down, I should see legs and bodies <u>walking</u> ... I'm not seeing any legs walking ... I'm not ...

(*She blasts the whistle again, this time directly into the bull horn. This seems to do the trick. She is now centerstage and stands on the cooler to address the group, still using the bull horn.*)

That's better. (*back to her "children's voice"*) Welcome, Sunday schoolers, to First Church's annual Easter Egg Hunt out here on the church's beautiful front lawn. I know you're all going to be on your very best behavior and not make too much noise and disturb the big 11:00 service inside, because if you do, Pastor Al may have to come out with his big, bad, frowny face and tell you to be quiet, and then Miss Yackanelli will have to wear her bigger, badder frowny face, and the Easter Bunny doesn't want frowny faces on Easter, now does he? All right, now if you're a bunny, raise your hand ... Good! And where are all the chickies? All right, bunnies over here (*indicates her L*). That's right, now ... wait a minute, stop shoving, chickies, or you'll have to go to the time-out coop ... (*she stops as she sees a hand; she sighs*) <u>Yes</u> Nathan, what is it?(*pause*) Yes, Nathan, you must be a bunny or a chickie. (*pause*) No, you don't have a choice, it's bunny or chickie. (*pause, her irritation grows*) Bunny or chickie, Nathan, (*pause, almost yelling*) No, you cannot be a raptor. You're poultry, hang a left. (*to the group*) Baskets ready? Now when I count three, everyone run and find all those eggs ... (*quickly, as an afterthought*) ... just stay out of the Mary-Martha-Circle's pansy and snapdragon beds ... and, onnneee— twwwoooo—

(*She stops, looking out at the group that has obviously just run off. She sighs, drops the bull horn, and says in her regular voice —*)

Happy hunting. (*She steps off the cooler and walks to the lawn chair*) Next year, Gloria gets to do this. I'm going to make sure she gets a "calling."

(*She sits in a chair, plops her shoes off, and props her feet up on the cooler. She takes a chocolate bunny from her basket and prepares to eat when she notices TAYLOR walk on. He is engrossed in his Gameboy. She watches him a moment, then speaks*)

Taylor, what are you doing?

(*No response; he continues to play. She tries again, louder.*)

Why aren't you out with the others, Taylor?

(*Still no reply. She picks up her bull horn and broadcasts directly at him.*)

TAYLOR BRADLEY!!

(*TAYLOR jumps, quite startled, and obviously makes a mistake in his game.*)

TAYLOR: Ohhh maaannnn . . . I was almost to Chocolate Island and now Luigi loses Yoshi <u>and</u> gets nuked by a fireball.

MISS YACKANELLI: (*totally deadpan*) My condolences.

TAYLOR: And I had star power too. (*starts to punch the game again*) It's back to Yoshi's Island . . . maaannnn . . .

MISS YACKANELLI: (*standing and walking to him*) Taylor, could you put that piece of silicone away for a minute. I need to ask you an important question. Now . . . are you a bunny or a chickie?

(*TAYLOR gives her a long "Oh pluheeze" look.*)

All right, forget the livestock. Why aren't you hunting eggs?

TAYLOR: I'm a conscientious objector.

MISS YACKANELLI: Taylor, it's Easter morning! The Easter bunny came before you got up this morning and left all these yummy eggs . . . and candy and . . . (*she stops, seeing TAYLOR's look*) I, uh, see we're harboring a few doubts about the Easter bunny . . .

TAYLOR:	Look Miss Yackanelli, no offense, but this Easter bunny thing is probably the most insulting sham ever forced on kids.
MISS YACKANELLI:	(*taken aback*) Oh?
TAYLOR:	I mean, think about it. A giant rabbit—a species that has no frontal vision, no memory, and whose IQ is only one notch above the armadillo. This rabbit—whose best time is just barely 18 MPH—still manages to visit every house in the country. He covers all terrain vertically, hopping on his back legs—a position in which no rabbit has ever been observed moving. Then, with paws, he bypasses home security systems and not only delivers, but hides eggs—chicken eggs—in living rooms. And not once has he been arrested, shot at . . . or appeared on AMERICA'S MOST WANTED. (*pause*) Go figure.
	(*TAYLOR goes back to his Gameboy. MISS YACKANELLI stares at him for a moment.*)
MISS YACKANELLI:	(*again deadpan*) Is that all?
TAYLOR:	(*without looking up*) Yeah. Except that I'm sure he's illegally distributing those marshmallow chicks. Even the FDA couldn't have approved those. Major gag.
MISS YACKANELLI:	Uh huh.
TAYLOR:	Yep. (*sigh*) Another kid's holiday bites the dust.
MISS YACKANELLI:	What do you mean?
TAYLOR:	Well, once the bunny myth explodes, there's not much left of Easter . . . for kids, I mean.
	(*MISS YACKANELLI has been studying TAYLOR. When she talks, her voice is now more adult.*)
MISS YACKANELLI:	Taylor . . . (*he looks up; she motions to a lawn chair*) Park it here. (*he walks over to the chair and sits*) We need to have some words about Easter. (*she begins to rummage around in her wicker basket*)
TAYLOR:	Miss Yackanelli, I didn't mean it was bad or nothin' . . .
MISS YACKANELLI:	All right. I want you to think about Easter as . . . (*she holds up a dyed egg*) . . . this egg. On the outside, Easter may seem painted and artificial, but on the inside, it's made up of . . .
TAYLOR:	. . . cholesterol?

(*A pause. MISS YACKANELLI looks at TAYLOR.*)

MISS YACKANELLI: OK. Let's try this again. (*she tosses the egg in the basket and pulls out a chocolate bunny*) Now . . . Easter is like this chocolate bunny. On the outside it's covered with bright, shiny colors, but on the inside it's . . .

TAYLOR: . . . hollow?

(*MISS YACKANELLI looks at TAYLOR again.*)

MISS YACKANELLI: This isn't going the way it's supposed to. (*she looks in the basket once more*)

TAYLOR: I think I've seen one too many of Pastor Al's children's sermons with the mystery box . . .

MISS YACKANELLI: Ah hah, ah hah! Here it is. Easter is like . . .

(*She holds up a marshmallow chick. They both look at it. Pause. Then they both speak together—*)

BOTH: Major gag.

(*MISS YACKANELLI tosses the chick back in the basket.*)

MISS YACKANELLI: All right, let's forget the object lessons. (*TAYLOR pulls out his Gameboy*) And let's not forget this object too. (*she takes the game and puts it on the cooler*) You know, the object Easter is really about you can't see.

TAYLOR: Yeah?

MISS YACKANELLI: Yeah. It's right here.

(*She points at his chest. TAYLOR looks confused and takes a wad of chewed gum out of his front shirt pocket.*)

TAYLOR: Bubble gum?

MISS YACKANELLI: No, inside, Taylor. (*he looks at her*) Easter's about love.

TAYLOR: (*Shaking his head*) Nah, that doesn't seem quite right, Miss Yackanelli.

MISS YACKANELLI: What do you think of?

TAYLOR: (*more serious*) Well what I think of doesn't seem quite right either.

MISS YACKANELLI: (*gently*) And what's that?

TAYLOR: (*quietly*) Death.

MISS YACKANELLI:	(*nodding*) Yes, that is part of Easter.
TAYLOR:	I know I'm supposed to think about the empty tomb and that He rose from the dead and is alive . . . but I just keep thinking about how Jesus died. It's what I always think about when Easter comes up. (*pause*) Maybe that's why I kinda avoid it. It makes me feel bad.
MISS YACKANELLI:	It's OK to feel bad, Taylor. Everybody felt bad when Jesus died—especially His heavenly Father. But that's how I know Easter is about love—because of how Jesus died.
TAYLOR:	I don't understand . . .
MISS YACKANELLI:	I'm not sure any of us fully understands, but I do know this. I know that God made us and loves us very much—so much, in fact, that although we keep turning our backs on Him and sinning, and so deserve to die, God couldn't bear to let that happen. So He sent His Son—His only Son—to die in our place. And Jesus went to His death <u>knowing</u> that. He went willingly, knowing that through His death, we could be made right with God again. * (*pause*) Does that make sense?
TAYLOR:	Sorta.
MISS YACKANELLI:	Let me try to explain it another way.
TAYLOR:	You're not gonna use the jelly beans, are you . . . ?
MISS YACKANELLI:	(*smiling*) No. I'm going to use <u>you</u>. Let's say you did something you knew was very wrong and your dad found out about it. Let's say you broke a window with a baseball and someone had to pay to replace it. And although you knew you were to blame and should be punished, another kid—someone you hardly knew—stepped in and took your punishment and worked to pay the price of fixing the window. What would you say about a kid like that?
TAYLOR:	I'd say he was crazy.
MISS YACKANELLI:	Yes, a lot of people said that about Jesus. In fact, much of the world still says that about Him. But what would you say about what He did for you?
TAYLOR:	I'd say I didn't really understand why He did it . . .
MISS YACKANELLI:	Yes. And . . .
TAYLOR:	And I'd say He must like me for some reason. A lot.
MISS YACKANELLI:	(*smiling*) Yes. A lot. **

* *At this point, MISS YACKANELLI could sing "Oh, How He Loves You and Me" if desired. An underscore of the tune could continue through the end of the sketch.*

** *At this point, TAYLOR and MISS YACKANELLI could sing the chorus again. If the congregation joined them on the repeat, it would be very effective.*

O Sacred Head, Now Wounded

TEXT: Paul Gerhardt; based on a Medieval Latin poem ascribed to Bernard of Clairvaux; translated from the German by James W. Alexander

MUSIC: Hans Leo Hassler; harmonized by J.S. Bach

The complete story of this chorale/hymn is told in Phil Lollar's interesting sketch that follows.

This piece is certainly one of the finest pieces of music in all hymnals, and contains a dual dignity and passion that is moving and unique. Bach's harmonization captures the beauty and sadness of the cross in a profound way.

O sacred Head, now wounded,
With grief and shame weighed down,
Now scornfully surrounded
With thorns Thine only crown:
How pale Thou art with anguish,
With sore abuse and scorn,
How does that visage languish,
Which once was bright as morn!

What Thou, my Lord, hast suffered
Was all for sinners' gain;
Mine, mine was the transgression,
But Thine the deadly pain.
Lo, here I fall, my Savior;
'Tis I deserve Thy place;
Look on me with Thy favor,
Assist me with Thy grace.

What language shall I borrow
to thank Thee, dearest Friend,
For this, Thy dying sorrow,
Thy pity without end?
O make me Thine forever,
And should I fainting be,
Lord, let me never, never
Outlive my love to Thee.

O Sacred Head, Now Wounded
A Dramatic Sketch
by Phil Lollar

SYNOPSIS
A mock news report on the many men responsible for bringing us the hymn "O Sacred Head, Now Wounded." ** NOTE: This piece can be sung by a small Ensemble or Church Choir. Also, you can try the foreign accents if you are brave. Otherwise, regular strong, clear speaking voices are fine.

| Performance Time: | Approximately 10 minutes, with hymn |

WORSHIP USES
Palm Sunday; Holy Week; any service where this hymn is used.

WORD MUSIC RESOURCES
- Brass Choir, arr. by Anita Kerr, #301601131X
- Studio Series Artist Trax, as recorded by First Call, #3017521206

SETTING/PROPS
Modern chair, small table and chair, quill pen, pieces of music on parchment, church organ.

CHARACTERS
ANNOUNCER-	offstage voice
CHET HINKLEY-	news anchor
BERNARD-	abbot of Clairveaux, author of the text
HANS LEO HASSLER-	composer of the tune
PAUL GERHARDT-	German translator of the text
J. S. BACH-	harmonization composer
JAMES ALEXANDER-	English translator of the text
SINGERS	

(*We start with the choir/ensemble singing the first verse of "O Sacred Head, Now Wounded."*)

SINGERS: O sacred head, now wounded, with grief and shame weighed down,
Now scornfully surrounded with thorns Thine only crown,
How art Thou pale with anguish, with sore abuse and scorn!
How does that visage languish, which once was bright as morn!

(*As they sing, the lights go down completely on the stage and in the auditorium. Once the verse is finished, we hear the voice of an announcer out of the darkness.*)

ANN'CER: We interrupt this service to bring you a special report from Church History News. And now, here's Chet Hinkley.

(*Lights rise on stage right. There, CHET HINKLEY sits in a chair, his notes in front of him. He has the typical sense of self-importance and pomposity that most news anchors have, and he talks to us as though we were the camera.*)

CHET: Thank you. The Passion of Christ—the greatest single event in history. That moment in time when God became a man, and allowed Himself to be sacrificed by His creations so that those creations might live forever with Him. As we pause to reflect on the death, crucifixion and resurrection of our Lord, the event takes on an even greater significance when we stop to think of our forefathers who kept this heritage alive through song, and in doing so, made it possible for us to enjoy that heritage today, and in turn, pass it on to our children. Today, via time-travel satellite, we're going to talk with the men responsible for bringing us the hymn we just heard, "O Sacred Head, Now Wounded." We take you first to a monastery in 12th-century France, where the author of the song's text lived.

(*During this last sentence, the lights fade on him and rise stage left where a peaceful, middle-aged monk kneels praying. He wears the traditional monk's robe.*)

CHET: Bernard? Bernard of Clairveaux, this is Chet Hinkley from Church History News. Are you there?

(*The monk finishes praying, then rises and turns to the audience. He looks at the audience through the entire interview.*)

BERNARD: Yes, my son. I was just finishing my prayers.

CHET: Pardon us. We didn't mean to interrupt.

BERNARD: No, no—you're not interrupting. Did you say that you're from "Church History News"?

CHET: That's right.

BERNARD: Then you are not of my time?

CHET: No, sir, I'm from the 20th century.

BERNARD: Twentieth?! Praise be to God that men still worship Him!

CHET: Part of the reason we are able to worship Him is because of people like you, Bernard, and that's what we're here to examine. You were born into a noble family at Fontaine-in-Burgundy, were you not?

BERNARD: Yes. My father was a knight and my mother a maiden of exceeding goodness.

CHET: But your life took a much different path.

BERNARD: Yes. I felt God's calling while still very young, and accepted the life of a monk.

CHET: A life at which you excelled. Modern scholars hold you to be one of the finest and most influential leaders of your time. Your life was dedicated to holiness, simplicity, devotion, prayer, preaching, and ministering to the physical and spiritual needs of others.

BERNARD: I am a sinner on whom God has seen fit to bestow His grace and mercy—nothing more, nothing less.

CHET: Tell us about the hymn, "O Sacred Head, Now Wounded."

BERNARD: I'm afraid I don't know what that is.

CHET: Oh, of course—you would only know it in Latin . . . (*consults his notes*) Um, the seventh part of the RHYTHMICA ORATORIO.

BERNARD: Ah! Salve Caput Cruentatum! (*pronounced: "SAHL-vey CAH-poot crew-en-TAH-toom."*)

CHET: Yes.

BERNARD: Well, the RHYTHMICA is a long poem in seven parts, each part addressing various members of Christ's body as He suffered on the cross: His feet, knees, hands, side, breast, heart, and face. That which you call "O Sacred Head, Now Wounded" came from the seventh portion of the poem. It was written to make us feel the passion of our Lord as He died for our sins. "O sacred head, now wounded, with grief and shame weighed down . . ." Excuse me, but did you call it a hymn?

CHET: Yes, I did.

BERNARD: And you still sing it in the 20th century?

CHET: We do.

BERNARD: To what music?

(*As CHET speaks, the lights dim on BERNARD and rise centerstage on a man, late 30s, dressed in a powdered wig [if you can get one] and a puffy shirt, sitting at a small table, scribbling furiously.*)

CHET: For that part of the story, we must use the time-travel satellite to jump forward nearly 500 years to the beginning of the seventeenth century. The year is 1610; the country is Germany; and the man behind the table is one of the finest German composers of the late Renaissance in both secular and sacred music. His name is Hans Leo Hassler. Herr Hassler?

HASSLER: (*not looking up*) Yes, yes, what is it?

CHET: Chet Hinkley, Church History News. We are here to talk to you about a piece of music you wrote.

HASSLER: (*still not looking up*) I've written many pieces of music. You'll have to be more specific than that.

CHET: We're interested in the music to one of your hymns.

(*HASSLER looks up and out at the audience. He also does not look at either CHET or BERNARD throughout the rest of the interview.*)

HASSLER: Hymns? I have written no hymns.

CHET: Are you certain? It's known as the "Passion Chorale." The melody goes like this:

(*He nods to a pianist or a soloist, who plays/sings the melody of "O Sacred Head, Now Wounded." Once the music is complete, HASSLER starts chuckling.*)

HASSLER: That tune is now a hymn?

CHET: Yes, sir, one of our most sacred.

HASSLER: God does indeed work in mysterious ways . . . That tune was originally a love song called "My Heart Is Distracted by a Gentle Maid." I published it in a collection of works in 1601.

(*The lights come back up on BERNARD*)

BERNARD: A love song? How wonderful!

CHET: Hans Leo Hassler, meet Bernard of Clairveaux, the monk who wrote the text of the hymn.

HASSLER: How do you do?

BERNARD: Very well, my son. But I am a bit confused. How did my verse, written in Latin, end up in Germany?

CHET:	For the answer, we must move forward in time nearly 50 years to Saxony, Germany, and bring on our next guest—a man recognized as one of the foremost hymnodists of the seventeenth century. Paul Gerhardt, are you there?
	(*The lights dim on BERNARD and HASSLER and rise on PAUL GERHARDT, middle-aged, also in a powdered wig [if you can get one], a puffy shirt and knee-high pants. He is looking over some music. He also looks straight out at the audience throughout the entire interview.*)
GERHARDT:	Yes, I am.
CHET:	Chet Hinkley, Church History News. You translated Bernard of Clairveaux's text, did you not?
GERHARDT:	I did. The "Salve Caput Cruentatum" is a most moving piece of work.
BERNARD:	Thank you, my son. God be praised.
GERHARDT:	Who is that?
CHET:	Bernard of Clairveaux.
GERHARDT:	An honor, sir!
HASSLER:	This is Hans Leo Hassler. How did you come to use my tune for this work?
GERHARDT:	What German does not know of the works of Hassler? My translation fit so well with your music, it was as if they were written for each other. And apparently, many in the church agreed, for the hymn was published in our famous hymnal, *Praxis Pietatis Melica* (PRONOUNCED: "PRAX-is Pie-TA-tis MEL-ih-cah") in 1656 and became an instant favorite.
CHET:	But you're not simply a translator, are you, Herr Gerhardt?
GERHARDT:	No, I've written a few hymns of my own.
CHET:	A few? You are credited with writing 132 hymn texts—texts which reflect an inner spiritual wealth, written under circumstances which would have made most men cry rather than sing: your childhood suffering during the Thirty Years' War; the loss of your wife and four children.
GERHARDT:	That is why I draw such comfort from "To the Suffering Face."
CHET:	"To the Suffering Face?"
GERHARDT:	That is what I call my translation: "To the Suffering Face of Jesus Christ."

CHET:	Hm . . . well, this medieval poem, written in Latin by a Frenchman, translated into German and set to the tune of a love song went through yet another important enhancement. We now move forward another 60 years to the Germany of the early 1700s. It was then that one of the most famous composers in history lived and worked—Johann Sebastian Bach, welcome to Church History News.
	(*During the above, the lights dim on BERNARD, HASSLER and GERHARDT, and rise on the organ where sits none other than JOHANN SEBASTIAN BACH. He, too, is dressed in a puffy shirt and powdered wig, and looks out at the audience, not at the others through the entire interview.*)
BACH:	Thank you!
CHET:	You are responsible for the harmonization of the "Passion Chorale," are you not, sir?
BACH:	Yes, I am.
HASSLER:	Harmonization?
BACH:	Who is there?
CHET:	That is Hans Leo Hassler, the composer of the tune.
BACH:	This is truly an honor, sir! Your tune is a masterpiece of simplicity and sadness—"passion" is the only word that can describe it!
HASSLER:	Thank you, but, what of this "harmonization?" May I hear it?
BACH:	Of course, of course!
	(*BACH [or the church organist] plays a verse of "O Sacred Head" with full harmonization.*)
HASSLER:	Magnificent!
BACH:	I am honored, sir, that you think my meager additions do your tune justice.
CHET:	As a matter of fact, Herr Bach, the tune is a favorite of yours, isn't it?
BACH:	Indeed it is. I used it or variations of it five times in my work, ST. MATTHEW PASSION.
CHET:	Why do you like it so?

BACH: Because it fits my main criterion for composition. You see, I believe that the aim and final reason of all music should be nothing else but the glory of God and the refreshment of the spirit.

CHET: Is that why many of your works begin with the inscription, "Jesus, help me!" and end with, "To God alone be the praise"?

BACH: Yes, it is.

HASSLER: Well, I hate to tell you, Herr Bach, but the tune started out as a secular love song.

BACH: Perhaps . . . but God had **greater** designs for it, my friend.

CHET: Well, this is all fascinating. And yet, for us, there is still a missing piece—the English translation to the hymn we sing today. For that, we must again move forward, this time to the year 1830. The place: America. And the translator: James W. Alexander. Mr. Alexander, are you there?

(*Lights dim on all the others and rise on JAMES W. ALEXANDER, mid-20s. He is wearing a pre-civil war frock coat and top hat, stands right centerstage, and also looks straight out at the audience.*)

JAMES: I am.

CHET: You taught history yourself, didn't you?

JAMES: Yes, sir, I did, at Princeton Theological Seminary. That is where I first came across, "To the Suffering Face of Jesus Christ" and the "Passion Chorale."

CHET: What made you think of translating it?

JAMES: I've always maintained an interest in hymnology, especially in translating early Latin and German texts. So, while pastoring a large Presbyterian church in New York, I thought of how wonderful it would be for my congregation to sing this hymn in their own tongue. The translation was instantly successful, and the hymn was published in the *Christian Lyre* hymnal.

CHET: Why do you think it is so popular?

JAMES: Because it speaks to the part of each of us that recognizes the truth of Jesus' death, burial and resurrection. In this song, we understand just what our Lord suffered in our place. We realize that we should have borne the crown of thorns . . . our heads should have been wounded . . . we should have been weighed down with grief, shame and scorn.

CHET: (*thoughtfully*) Mm . . . well, I want to thank all of you gentlemen for being with us today.

ALL: (*ad lib*) Thank you, Chet./ Herr Chet./ My son.

(*The lights fade on all of the historical figures and rise on CHET. The choir starts humming "O Sacred Head, Now Wounded."*)

CHET: Philip Schaff has said of "O Sacred Head, Now Wounded," "This classic hymn has shown in three tongues—Latin, German, and English—with equal effect, the dying love of our Savior and our boundless indebtedness to Him." Indeed, this one hymn <u>does</u> convey the astounding depth of our Savior's love, mercy and grace. It begs the question: How can one listen to it and not respond? (*pause*) For Church History News, I'm Chet Hinkley. We now return you to your regular service.

(*The lights dim on CHET and rise on the CHOIR/ENSEMBLE who start singing the second verse of "O Sacred Head, Now Wounded."*)

SINGERS: What Thou, my Lord, hast suffered was all for sinners' gain:
Mine, mine was the transgression, but Thine the deadly pain.
Lo, here I fall, my Savior! 'Tis I deserve Thy place;
Look on me with Thy favor, vouchsafe to me Thy grace.

(*And on the third verse, the lights rise on the congregation and the choir director/worship leader asks them to join in.*)

ALL: What language shall I borrow to thank Thee, dearest Friend,
For this Thy dying sorrow, Thy pity without end?
O make me Thine forever! And, should I fainting be,
Lord, let me never, never outlive my love to Thee!

Softly and Tenderly

TEXT and MUSIC: Will L. Thompson

This emotional hymn was written during the camp meeting-revival era of the late 19th century. It is a classic "invitation" text, inviting the listener to answer the call to Christ.

The hymn first appeared in a collection entitled, *Sparkling Gems, Nos. 1 & 2 Combined,* 1880. This collection was published by Thompson himself.

Softly and tenderly Jesus is calling,
Calling for you and for me;
See, on the portals He's waiting and watching,
Watching for you and for me.

REFRAIN:
Come home, come home,
Ye who are weary, come home;
Earnestly, tenderly, Jesus is calling,
Calling, O sinner, come home!

Why should we tarry when Jesus is pleading,
Pleading for you and for me?
Why should we linger and heed not His mercies,
Mercies for you and for me?

Time is now fleeting, the moments are passing,
Passing from you and from me;
Shadows are gathering, death beds are coming,
Coming for you and for me.

O for the wonderful love He has promised,
Promised for you and for me!
Though we have sinned, He has mercy and pardon,
Pardon for you and for me.

Softly and Tenderly
A Dramatic Sketch
by Phil Lollar

SYNOPSIS
An elderly saint tries to convince his/her equally elderly friend that Jesus' love and grace is always available, even in our twilight years.

| Performance Time: | Approximately 8 minutes with hymn |

WORSHIP USES
General worship services

WORD MUSIC RESOURCES
- 3-5 Octave Handbells, arr. by R. Lyndell Littleton, #3014094315

SETTING/PROPS
Two rocking chairs, centerstage

CHARACTERS
ROSCOE- Late 60s or older
HUBERT- Late 60s or older

NOTE: This sketch can also be performed by two women, Gertrude and Florence, or by a man and woman. It also doesn't have to be performed by older people—it can be done by younger people playing older. Your choice.

SINGERS

(*Lights rise on a couple of rocking chairs, center. One of them is empty. The other is occupied by an elderly man named ROSCOE. He doesn't rock or move for that matter, but looks straight ahead. After a few seconds, another elderly gentleman, HUBERT, enters, holding a letter. He walks over to ROSCOE.*)

HUBERT: (*looks at the letter, happily*) This is great, this is just great! Hey, Roscoe, you wanna hear something funny? (*no answer*) I said, you wanna hear something funny? (*no answer; he looks at ROSCOE*) Roscoe? (*a bit frightened*) Uh-oh . . . Roscoe, buddy?

(*Suddenly, ROSCOE snores. HUBERT gives the audience an Oliver Hardy take, then nudges ROSCOE*) Roscoe!

ROSCOE: (*awakens and yells out*) B-29! I-47! N-17! G-32—

HUBERT: (*above him*) Whoa, whoa! Hold it! Wait! <u>Hold it</u>!

ROSCOE: (*stops*) What? Hubert! What is it?

HUBERT: We're past that.

ROSCOE: Past what?

HUBERT: The afternoon bingo game.

ROSCOE: We are?

HUBERT: Yep.

ROSCOE: Completely past?

HUBERT: Yep.

ROSCOE: What'd I miss?

HUBERT: You won.

ROSCOE: Rats! I <u>hate</u> it when that happens! . . . Sorry.

HUBERT: S'all right.

ROSCOE: Was I asleep?

HUBERT: Yep.

ROSCOE: Did I snore?

HUBERT: Yep.

ROSCOE: Drool?

HUBERT: (*looks*) Nope.

ROSCOE: Well, that's <u>something,</u> at least . . .

(*HUBERT sits in the other rocker.*)

HUBERT: Listen, I have something I want to read to you.

ROSCOE: Yeah? What?

HUBERT: Oh, it's this funny thing. I copied it down this morning at church. It's a letter from a college student to her parents . . . (*reads*) "Dear Mom and Dad, I realize it's been a while since I've written to you, so I just want to start this letter off by saying that I'm all right and there's nothing for you to worry about—I got out of the dorm before it burned down . . ."

ROSCOE: You call that funny?

HUBERT: Hold on . . . (*reads*) "But to get out, I had to jump out of the window, which, as you know, is on the second floor. Fortunately, there were several old boxes under my window, and they broke my fall—well, they and my arm, which I also broke . . ."

ROSCOE: Good grief!

HUBERT: (*reads on*) "Everybody was too busy fighting the fire to call me an ambulance, so I ran across the street to the gas station to use the phone there. Only I didn't have a quarter, so the attendant, Mike, took me to the hospital. On the way, we started talking, and it dawned on me that, now that the dorm burned down, I didn't have a place to live. But Mike came to my rescue and said that I could stay with him, so that's where I've lived for the past few months . . ."

ROSCOE: You're kidding!

HUBERT: There's more . . . (*reads*) "I think you'll like Mike—he's a real nice guy—when he's sober. And I think he'll make a great father . . . Yes, Mom and Dad, I'm pregnant."

ROSCOE: This is too much!

HUBERT: Wait, here's the last paragraph. (*reads*) "Well, folks, I'd better close. Oh, by the way, none of the above is true. The dorm is still here, I'm still living in it, my arm is fine, I'm not pregnant and I don't even know any boys named Mike. But I am getting a D in math, and I sure could use some more money. Love, your daughter."

ROSCOE: (*chuckles*) Clever! Very clever!

HUBERT: (*also chuckles*) Yeah. Kinda puts your problems in perspective, doesn't it?

ROSCOE: Uh-huh . . . Where'd you say you got that?

HUBERT: At church this morning. It was part of the Pastor's sermon.

ROSCOE: Church? Doesn't sound like any sermon I've ever heard.

HUBERT: Well, the Pastor is always coming up with stuff like that.

ROSCOE: (*grunts*) Mm.

(*Slight pause.*)

HUBERT: (*lightly*) You ought to come and hear him next Sunday. I think you'd enjoy it.

ROSCOE: I knew it! You just can't resist, can you?

HUBERT: Resist what?

ROSCOE: Preaching at me! Trying to get me to go to church with you! You guys are all alike!

HUBERT: Whoa, whoa, whoa! I'm not preachin' at you! I just made a simple comment. If you don't want to go to church, that's your business.

ROSCOE: Thank you very much!

(*Another pause.*)

HUBERT: Why <u>don't</u> you want to go to church?

ROSCOE: I knew it! I knew it!

HUBERT: I'm your friend! I'm curious! Sue me! I happen to think going to church is very important! I didn't know there were subjects we can't discuss!

ROSCOE: There aren't any subjects we can't discuss . . . Look, I just don't like those kind of people, you know?

HUBERT: Wait a minute—<u>I'm</u> one of "those kind of people."

ROSCOE: You know what I mean! I'm talking about people who say "Praise the Lord," all the time, and fall down on their knees in prayer every ten minutes and lift their hands up to the sky. And while they got their hands up there, the preacher's got <u>his</u> in their pockets!

HUBERT: Where'd you get that idea?

ROSCOE: I read the papers! I watch the news!

HUBERT: Let me get this straight:<u>You</u>—Mister "I-Don't-Trust-the-Media"—suddenly believes everything he reads and sees when it comes to church, is that it?

ROSCOE: (*sheepishly*) Well . . . no . . .

HUBERT: So, why don't you wanna come?

ROSCOE: (*a new tact*) I'm just not a "joiner," you know that. I've never been the kind to join clubs or groups.

HUBERT: What are you talking about? You used to belong to a church.

ROSCOE: That was a long time ago.

HUBERT: So? Besides, I don't recall asking you to <u>join</u> anything.

ROSCOE: I know how those places operate! They get you inside and make you fill out a "visitor's form" and the next thing you know, they're sending you mail and everybody's coming to your house and . . . and then you're hooked!!

HUBERT: In the first place, nobody is gonna make you fill out anything you don't want to fill out. And in the second place, we're talking about going to church! You make it sound like an addiction or something!

ROSCOE: I've seen those cult groups! I'll end up standing on a corner with my head shaved, trying to sell flowers to parked cars!

(*There is a long pause as HUBERT stares at ROSCOE.*)

HUBERT: You aren't serious, are you?

ROSCOE: (*smiles*) No.

HUBERT: Good! For a minute there, I thought I was going to have to check your medication!

ROSCOE: Hubert . . . the truth is, I've thought about going back to church.

HUBERT: Then why don't you?

ROSCOE: I just don't think it's for me anymore.

HUBERT: It was once—it can be again.

ROSCOE: No.

HUBERT: Why not? . . . (*a pause; gently*) Roscoe, why not?

ROSCOE: I . . . God . . . won't have me anymore.

HUBERT: What?

ROSCOE: God won't have me anymore.

HUBERT: Oh, yes, He will—

ROSCOE: No! He won't . . . (*he takes a deep breath*) When Peg died . . . I was very angry . . . I felt betrayed by God . . . I needed His comfort and I didn't feel it . . . I just felt pain. . . . One afternoon, something snapped. I stood up, shook my fist toward heaven and cursed God.

HUBERT: That was just your grief talking.

ROSCOE: No, it wasn't. I knew exactly what I was doing. I tore up every Bible in my house . . . and then I threw them out. I didn't want anything to do with God. How can I go back after that?

HUBERT: How can you _not_?

ROSCOE: Hubert—

HUBERT: Roscoe, do you think Jesus died for _perfect_ people? He died for _sinners_! For the dregs of the earth! Even for people who reject Him. You know, the folks who crucified Him thought they knew what they were doing, too. And Jesus still said, "Father, forgive them."

ROSCOE: It's . . . been too long. There's no room for me anymore. It's too late.

(_pause_)

HUBERT: Roscoe, do you remember any of the stories from the Bible?

ROSCOE: Some.

HUBERT: Do you remember the one about the man who hired workers to work in his fields? He hired them at different times of the day—but when it came time to pay them, he gave them all the same amount of money—even the ones he had hired when the work was almost finished.

ROSCOE: I remember.

HUBERT: It doesn't matter how or when you come to Jesus, Roscoe, or how long it's been since you last saw Him . . . all that matters is that you _do_ come. Come home.

(_pause_)

ROSCOE: (_near tears_) I . . . do . . . want to . . . come home.

HUBERT: I know.

ROSCOE: (_a deep breath_) I guess it . . . wouldn't hurt to try church next Sunday.

HUBERT: (_smiles_) Wouldn't hurt at all. We could even go together if you want.

ROSCOE: I'd like that . . . (_beat_) Will I have to shave my head?

HUBERT: (_chuckles_) No.

ROSCOE: (*also chuckles; then*) Hubert?

HUBERT: Yeah?

ROSCOE: Do you think maybe we could . . . pray?

HUBERT: (*warmly*) Absolutely, my friend. Absolutely.

(*The two of them bow together, as the lights dim on them and rise on the ensemble or chorus, who sing "Softly and Tenderly" with or without the congregation.*)

Were You There?

TEXT and MUSIC:
Traditional Spiritual

Although African-American slaves were writing and creating spirituals in the pre-Civil War period, it wasn't until the later 1860s that they began to appear in print. The versions most commonly heard were European-arranged concert versions. The harmonies and rhythms of these arrangements are what appear in today's hymnals.

The pathos of the sentiment "causes me to tremble," along with the descending melodic line make this an affecting hymn. The spiritual itself is already dramatic. The addition of Lollar's Reader's Theater should provide a unique worship moment.

> Were you there when they crucified my Lord?
> Were you there when they crucified my Lord?
> O! Sometimes it causes me to tremble, tremble, tremble!
> Were you there when they crucified my Lord?
>
> Were you there when they nailed Him to the tree?
> Were you there when they nailed Him to the tree?
> O! Sometimes it causes me to tremble, tremble, tremble!
> Were you there when they nailed Him to the tree?
>
> Were you there when they laid Him in the tomb?
> Were you there when they laid Him in the tomb?
> O! Sometimes it causes me to tremble, tremble, tremble!
> Were you there when they laid Him in the tomb?
>
> Were you there when He rose up from the dead?
> Were you there when He rose up from the dead?
> O! Sometimes I feel like shouting glory, glory, glory!
> Were you there when He rose up from the dead?

Were You There?
A Brief Reader's Theatre
by Phil Lollar

SYNOPSIS
Four readers describe the Crucifixion and Resurrection, bringing it down to a personal plane. This piece can be done using a Quartet, a small Ensemble, the Church Choir or Congregational singing. For a different effect, try mixing-and-matching.

| Performance Time: | 5-7 minutes with hymn |

WORSHIP USES
Palm Sunday; Holy Week; Easter Sunday

WORD MUSIC RESOURCES
- Studio Series Artist Trax, as recorded by Russ Taff, #3017828204

SETTING/PROPS
The normal sanctuary stage. Four microphones and small podiums or music stands will be needed.

CHARACTERS
FOUR READERS—Any age.
SINGERS

*(At rise, the lights are up full on both the stage and in the house. The singers hum a verse of "Were You There?" as the FOUR READERS enter and take their places facing the congregation. **They are not in numerical order**, but are lined up as follows: READER THREE, READER ONE, READER FOUR, READER TWO. When they are in place, the lights dim in the sanctuary, leaving only the readers illuminated. The music leader then leads the SINGERS in the **first verse** of "Were You There?")*

SINGERS: Were you there when they crucified my Lord?
Were you there when they crucified my Lord?
O! Sometimes it causes me to tremble, tremble, tremble.
Were you there when they crucified my Lord?

READER 1: And the betrayer led the mob to Him as He was praying in the garden. His enemies had heard His words, but instead of love, the words filled them with hate, and they sought to put Him to death.

READER 2: There was no one to defend Him—even among His closest friends and followers. One betrayed Him . . . one denied Him . . . all ran away.

READER 3: He was tried before three separate courts: the High Priest . . . Pontius Pilate, the Roman Governor . . . and King Herod. All were mock trials—no reliable witness could be found against Him.

READER 4: And yet, Pilate gave in to the pressure from the crowd—incited by Herod and the High Priest—and ordered Jesus to be flogged . . . and then crucified.

READER 1: Just a week before, He had entered the city of Jerusalem triumphant!

READER 2: But now the shouts of "Hosanna! Glory and praise to God!" had turned to screams of "Crucify Him!"

READER 3: Crucify Him!

READER 4: Crucify Him!

READER 2: So they took Jesus, bearing His cross upon His back, to the place of the skull, which is called in Hebrew "Golgotha."

READER 3: And there, they crucified Him. And with Him, two others, one on either side, and Jesus between them.

READER 4: And Pilate wrote a title and put it on the cross; it read, "Jesus of Nazareth, the King of the Jews."

(SINGERS sing **verse two** of "Were You There?")

SINGERS: Were you there when they nailed Him to the tree?
Were you there when they nailed Him to the tree?
O! Sometimes it causes me to tremble, tremble, tremble.
Were you there when they nailed Him to the tree?

READER 1: My God, my God, why hast Thou forsaken Me?
O my God, I cry by day, but Thou dost not answer;
And by night, but I have no rest.
I am a worm, and not a man, a reproach of men,
and despised by the people.
All who see Me sneer at Me; they make mouths at Me,
they wag the head.

READER 2: He committed Himself to the Lord; let the Lord deliver Him!

(READER TWO turns away from the audience.)

READER 1: I am poured out like water, and all My bones are out of joint;
My heart is like wax; it is melted within Me.
My strength is dried up like a potsherd,
and My tongue cleaves to My jaws;
And Thou dost lay Me in the dust of death.

READER 3: Let the Lord rescue Him, for the Lord delights in Him!

(READER THREE turns away from the audience.)

READER 1: For dogs have surrounded Me; a band of evildoers has encompassed Me;
They pierced My hands and feet. I can count all My bones.
They look, they stare at Me; they divide My garments among them,
And for My clothing they cast lots.

READER 4: Come down off the cross if You are God's Son! You saved others—now save Yourself!

(*READER FOUR turns away from the audience.*)

READER 1: My God, My God, why hast Thou forsaken Me?

(*The lights fade on them. There is a pause, then from the darkness:*)

READER 2: And along with the mockers, there were those who mourned . . .

(*The lights on the readers rise. They now all have their backs to the audience. READER TWO turns to the audience and continues.*)

READER 2: Great Physician . . . it's me, the sick one . . . You cured me . . . and now You suffer a greater pain than ever I felt.

(*READER THREE turns to the audience and continues.*)

READER 3: Rabbi . . . it is I, the seeker of truth . . . You gave me the words of life, the message of hope, the promise of eternity . . . and even in death, You still give the greatest gift: Yourself.

(*READER FOUR turns to the audience and continues.*)

READER 4: Master . . . it's me, Your disciple . . . How often have I run from You . . . and betrayed You . . . and now, the ultimate betrayal: You hang on a Cross . . . dying in my place.

(*READER ONE turns to the audience and continues.*)

READER 1: Savior . . . it is I, the sinner . . . You, who knew no sin, have become sin . . . *my* sin . . . that I might be saved.

READER 2: Is there a sorrow deeper than this?

READER 3: Is there a death less deserved?

READER 4: Has a greater price ever been paid?

(*A pause*)

READER 1: And when Jesus had spoken His last, He bowed His head, and gave up the Spirit.

READER 3: He was the spotless Lamb—the perfect sacrifice . . . Jesus Christ took the weight of the sins of the world—*our* sins—upon Himself.

READER 4: He died in our place—each of us deserved to be on that cross.

READER 2: But God loved the world so much, He gave His only Son to die that we might be saved. God sacrificed Himself *to* Himself for us . . .

(*SINGERS sing **verse three** of "Were You There?"*)

SINGERS: Were you there when they laid Him in the Tomb?
Were you there when they laid Him in the Tomb?
O! Sometimes it causes me to tremble, tremble, tremble.
Were you there when they laid Him in the Tomb?

READER 1: After He died, a man named Joseph of Arimathea went to Pilate and asked for the body. He took it down and washed it and wrapped it in a linen cloth and laid Him in a sepulchre cut into the side of a mountain, where no one had ever lain.

READER 4: Mary, His mother, and the women who had come with Him from Galilee, followed.

READER 2: His followers huddled together in a small house in Jerusalem. For three days, they clung to each other, helpless, afraid.

READER 3: Memories of Him flooded every mind . . . He was going to usher in the new Kingdom—make Israel a great nation once again and wipe the Roman scourge from the earth . . . And now He was dead.

READER 4: Their grief was overwhelming. And they grieved not just for *Him*, but for themselves—for when you lose something very precious, you don't mourn just for the thing lost, you mourn for *you*.

READER 1: "With all those miracles He could do," they thought, "could He not have reserved one for Himself?" . . . They did not realize that He had! For Himself, and for us as well, He reserved the greatest miracle of all!

READER 2: At dawn on the first day of the week, Mary Magdalene and the other Mary went to look in the tomb.

READER 3: There was a violent earthquake, for an angel of the Lord came down from heaven, and, going to the tomb, rolled back the stone that blocked the entrance.

READER 4: The angel's appearance was like lightning, and his clothes were white as snow. The guards posted at the tomb were so afraid of him, they shook and became like dead men . . .

READER 1: The angel said to the women, "Do not be afraid, for I know that you are looking for Jesus, Who was crucified. He is not here; He is risen, just as He said."

ALL: He is not here! He is risen! Alleluia!

*(SINGERS sing **verse four** of "Were You There?" If the congregation has not joined yet, they should definitely sing here.)*

SINGERS: Were you there when He rose up from the grave?
Were you there when He rose up from the grave?
O! Sometimes it causes me to tremble, tremble, tremble.
Were you there when He rose up from the grave?

When I Survey the Wondrous Cross

TEXT: Isaac Watts
MUSIC: Based on a Gregorian Chant; arranged by Lowell Mason

This classic text was written by Isaac Watts, regarded by historians as "the Father of English hymnody." This hymn is often noted as the greatest English hymn. The hymn was first published in 1707 in Watts' own collection entitled *Hymns and Spiritual Songs*, under the title "Crucifixion to the World, by the Cross of Christ." The text is based on Galatians 6:14.

The tune HAMBURG was written in 1824 in Savannah, Georgia. It was sung for the first time in the First Presbyterian Church in Savannah. The tune with Watts' text was first published in *The Boston Handel and Haydn Collection of Church Music*.

When I survey the wondrous cross
On which the Prince of Glory died,
My richest gain I count but loss,
And pour contempt on all my pride.

Forbid it, Lord, that I should boast,
Save in the death of Christ, my God;
All the vain things that charm me most—
I sacrifice them to His blood.

See from His head, His hands, His feet,
Sorrow and love flow mingled down;
Did e'er such love and sorrow meet,
Or thorns compose so rich a crown?

Were the whole realm of nature mine,
That were a present far too small:
Love so amazing, so divine,
Demands my soul, my life, my all.

When I Survey the Wondrous Cross
A Dramatic Sketch
by
Deborah Craig-Claar

SYNOPSIS
The stories of three believers from other countries who have suffered great physical and emotional persecution for their faith are related in dramatic monologues. In each case, the cross of Christ—in word, symbol, or object—provides strength and sustenance during their suffering. The stories are all based on actual testimonies of believers living in repressed countries during the past fifteen years. The dramatic pieces can be used separately or as a unit. They can be memorized and presented as dramatic characters, or they can be performed in a reader's theater style.

Performance Time: 3-4 minutes per testimony

WORSHIP USES
Palm Sunday; Good Friday; General use

If all the testimonies are used, it will be a 10—12 minute presentation. Therefore, it may be helpful to choose only one monologue a week over three weeks in the Easter season, or simply use only one monologue if you only have 3—4 minutes to work with. If there is time to use all three monologues, they could be divided up within the service, or each separate monologue could be followed by a stanza of the hymn. If the choir will be singing the hymn arrangement, it should follow the monologues.

WORD MUSIC RESOURCES
- SATB Anthem, arr. Fred C. Mallory, orch. Camp Kirkland, # 3010686161 *Choral Trax and Orchestration are available.*
- 4-5 Octave Handbells, arr. Barry Braman, # 3014079316

SETTING/PROPS
There is no specific setting. If you will be performing this piece as Reader's Theater, consider using black music stands to hold the scripts. The stands can be placed in a line or semicircle on the platform, or the individuals can be positioned throughout the sanctuary. Each character holds a single prop: a simple wooden cross made of two sticks and bound with a piece of cloth (Kahla), an old Bible (Sahid), and a bare tree branch, roughly in the shape of a cross.

CHARACTERS
KAHLA, a young Christian woman, a convert from Hinduism, living in Nepal

SAHID, a Christian student from Morocco, studying in Egypt

MARINA, a Christian mother living in The Czech Republic

If the characters are being performed dramatically, the actors should wear clothing characteristic of their country. If the pieces are being performed as Reader's Theater, the performers should wear generic dress—possibly all black or black and white.

NOTE:
The stories related in these monologues were adapted and dramatized from interviews recorded in Called To Suffer, Called To Triumph *by Herbert Schlosser, Multnomah Press, 1990. The character names used here are fictitious.*

KAHLA

It seems all I had ever known was fear. I was born in a tiny village in Western Nepal and my family and our entire community were Hindu. We lived in constant terror and supplication to the hundreds of Hindu gods. Every disease, every bit of weather, every misfortune was due to evil spirits—only prayers and animal sacrifices would mollify them. As a child, I can remember running from house to house because I was afraid of being exposed to an open sky. It seemed I always had a stomach ache.

Then after I was 18, I met a student from the University at Kathmandu. He told me about the gospel of Jesus Christ, but I had a hard time believing him. It is very difficult to accept a God of grace and peace when all you've ever known are gods of fear. But he gave me a New Testament and I began reading it. Slowly, the story of a man who loved me enough to die for me became real, and I secretly gave my life to Christ.

The student who had given me the Bible eventually became my husband, and we settled in my village. It's very isolated and you can only reach it by climbing over the mountains for a week.

I told my parents and my brothers and sisters I had become a Christian. At first they were horrified, then they were angry, and finally they became cold and silent. My father told me that I could never enter the house again—that I was a very low person, an outcast. "You have brought shame on the name of this family forever," he said, and shut the front door of his house to me—forever. Soon the word spread, and the whole community turned against us. To profess Christ is taken as a repudiation of one's family and neighbors. No children were allowed to play with ours. The town kept us from taking water from a common stream, thinking we would contaminate it. Whenever people enter the village, they read on large stones at the entrance who has become a Christian—so that they may avoid them. My family never came to physical harm, but several Christian friends of my husband from the University in another village were beaten; their houses were torn down and their crops were set on fire.

During those early days it seemed that the great peace I had found in Jesus began to crumble and crack and give way to the old fears. Many of the old questions returned. So did the stomach aches.

Then one day I was standing in my kitchen, beginning to prepare dinner. I looked at the table and started to cry as I had so many times, realizing I would never see my parents again. Then my eyes went to the empty shelf just above the table. In Hindu homes, this is where the idol of each family's particular god is kept, so that all food might be offered to it before it is eaten. Oh, how I can remember my mother pleading with me to put this ugly stone statue up there so that she could share the table with her grandchildren. But I had refused, and the shelf remained empty—a testament to my stubborn faith, and the empty space in my heart.

Then suddenly, my spirit lifted; it seemed as if God were urging me to fill it. I grabbed two small pieces of wood from the pile of kindling next to the stove, and quickly bound them together with a rag.

(*She slowly holds up the wooden cross in her hand.*)

I looked at it, and slowly my tears stopped, and then my fears went away. I stuck it in some wet clay and put it on the idol's shelf, where it's remained for nine years. It fills the room with strength and hope and light . . . and daily refills my heart with the love that casts out all fear.

SAHID

I could barely contain my excitement—I was being allowed to go to Egypt to receive discipleship training. I am Moroccan by birth and came to know Christ through missionaries when I was a child. But the religion of Morocco is Islam, and any Christian activity there is closed down immediately by police, and severe punishment is meted out. Although I knew there was also Christian persecution in Egypt—especially since the Islamic revolution in Iran—it was at least legal to profess Christ there. Or so I thought.

Three brothers and I had rented an apartment in Alexandria, where we were attending a small Bible training seminar. One night three men broke through the door, demanding to know what we were doing in Egypt. The men were police in civilian clothing, and once they saw the Christian books and papers, they stuffed them into suitcases and drug us to the police barracks.

For days and nights they would not let us sleep or eat. They ridiculed and interrogated us, asking question after question, always accompanied by slaps and kicking.

"What do you think of Christians?" an officer would ask.

"They are nice people," I would say.

"Are you saying Moslems are bad?!" and bang would come another hand across the face. They would beat us on the soles of our feet and make us run in place until we thought our feet would rupture with pain.

After three days we were taken to a political prison outside Cairo. We were incarcerated with members of the Moslem Brotherhood, the very men who had killed President Sadat. This was very dangerous for us, as the Brotherhood has a special hatred for Christians, especially those who convert from Islam.

We were packed together in tiny, dark cells. The air was always stale and full of mosquitos. For the first two months we could not bathe or brush our teeth. Our food was rice and beans and was always full of insects. Drinking water was contaminated by the hole in the floor that served as our toilet. We slept on the dirt floor.

After many months we began to lose all hope. Day after day we simply sat, staring at the walls. We had no Bible, no cross . . . not even a blanket. Many of us had not seen the sun for weeks. It was as if we were dying, slowly, just a little at a time.

One night, when all seemed darkest, a brother named Jabar began to slowly quote Bible verses. His low, broken voice cut through the cold and stench of the night: "I count all things to be loss in view of the surpassing value of knowing Jesus Christ my Lord, for whom I have suffered the loss of all things, and count them but rubbish in order that I may gain Christ."

Slowly, one by one, other voices called out: "Just as the sufferings of Christ are ours in abundance, so also our comfort is abundant in Christ!" and

"May it never be that I should boast, except in the cross of the Lord, through which the world has been crucified to me, and I to the world."

And suddenly, our spirits began to rise, and it was as though a mighty cross had been raised over us in that dark room. Someone traced a cross in the dirt floor with their finger. We huddled around it and began to sing. We sang every hymn we'd ever heard, and usually in several languages. When we ran out, we made up our own. And so we got through the darkness and pain of the nights, strengthened to face once again the darkness and pain of the days.

It would be two years until we were released. And although we never once had a blanket, or a cross, or a Bible (*he hugs the Bible to himself*) . . . the word and power of the risen Lord was with us—with<u>in</u> us—always.

MARINA

Nothing ever seems to stay the same. I've lived in Czechoslovakia over 40 years now and things are still changing. In Eastern Europe, whole countries disappear, then come back, then are carved up once again. When the Communist Party was still in control, you could never say what you believed—about religion, about politics, about anything. They say it's different now. But I'm still rising at 5:00 every morning, dropping off my children at school by 6:00 so I can be at the factory by 6:30. For the most part, we mothers have no choice about working. We can't live on one income and we cannot feed and clothe our children unless we work. It's so sad to see the buses every morning and every evening, crowded with exhausted women and crying children.

There have been many times I have not wanted my children in the schools, but what choice do I have? From kindergarten on they have been fed the Communist Party doctrine that Christianity is a religion of antiquated superstition. And since modern science can now explain the world, there is no longer any need for religion.

My children hear this all day, then come home each night to a Christian family. We pray, we worship, we read God's Word. We talk within our four walls about the truths in the gospel, but then we must ask our children to live a lie outside the walls. We tell our daughter she must give the teachers the answers they want, even if she doesn't believe it. For when a student says what they really believe, they may not be allowed to take the final exams or they may have to repeat a year of school. Our son used to always come home from school in tears, because he was bombarded with comments from the teachers that his family was backward and ignorant. We can go to church, but we can't talk about it. When we meet new people, we must never say we're Christians, for fear they'll get us in trouble—or that knowing us, we may some day get them in trouble. Our children have learned to be what is known in Czechoslovakia as "secret believers"—to have faith in their hearts, but not on their lips.

As I watched my daughter grow in her faith and into womanhood, she became increasingly heartsick with this demoralizing double life she was being asked to live. One winter afternoon as we walked through a public park, she talked about some beautiful medieval and Renaissance paintings she had seen in an art book in a museum. Wistfully, she decribed the beautiful gold and silver crosses that the clergy and the populace often wore around their necks.

"How I'd love to be able to do that," she said quietly. "How I'd love to wear His cross so everyone could see who I really am."

We both sat on a bench for a few minutes, sad and reflective, just staring up into the web of bare branches above us. And then, quite suddenly, I saw it—as clearly as if it were alone against the sky: (*she slowly raises the branch*) A cross, formed simply from two layered branches. I started to point it out to my daughter, but then I saw another one. Then another, and another . . . and it wasn't only the sky that they covered, but the ground as well. We didn't need to wear a cross—the world was wearing it for us.

It was a great lesson and a great comfort that we received that day. And now whenever we touch the earth, or search the sky . . . we need not be silent believers ever again.